I0460051

Life

But Make it Manageable

Tia Warrick

Copyright © 2025

All Rights Reserved

No part of this publication may be copied,
reproduced in any format, by any means, electronic or
otherwise, without prior consent from the copyright
owner and publisher of this book.

About the Author

Dr. Tia Warrick wears many hats—public health expert, clinical researcher, educator, and entrepreneur—but at her core, she's just someone trying to make life a little easier for herself and others. As the founder of Lesous Consulting LLC and an Assistant Professor of Biology, she's spent nearly a decade helping people untangle complicated health and career challenges. Through her work, she's learned that the secret to managing life isn't perfection—it's strategy. *Life, But Make It Manageable* is her way of sharing the practical, no-nonsense tools that have helped her (and countless others) navigate the chaos with a little more ease and a lot less stress.

Preface

There I was, hyperventilating.

I had done it again. I had let everything pile up, convincing myself that I could power through it all in just a few hours. I've always been good under pressure—at least, that's what I tell myself. I push deadlines, cram work into last-minute sprints, and assure myself that somehow, I'll pull it off like I always do. But this time, something felt different.

I wasn't just stressed—I was drowning.

I stared at my laptop, fingers frozen over the keyboard, but my brain wouldn't cooperate. I tried to will myself to move, to think, to start somewhere, but my body refused. My heart was racing, my breathing was shallow, and a wave of exhaustion slammed into me. The sheer weight of everything I had to do made me feel like I was sinking.

I kept saying, *just one task, just start with one thing.* But even that felt like too much.

And that's when the thought hit me.

Maybe the weight hasn't changed. Maybe I've just gotten weaker.

It wasn't an easy thing to admit. I used to be the kind of person who thrived on having a full plate—multiple jobs, school, deadlines, projects, commitments. I'd stack responsibility on top of responsibility, like I was proving something to myself. Proving I could handle it. Proving I could be everything to everyone. But somewhere along the way, I stopped bouncing back. What once felt like a challenge now felt like a punishment. Tasks that I could once knock out in an afternoon now drained me for days. And no amount of planning, scheduling, or pep talks could change the fact that I had nothing left to give.

Preface

I was completely, utterly, burnout.

At first, I thought I just needed to "get it together." That if I pushed through, worked harder, or managed my time better, I'd feel like myself again. But the more I tried to force productivity, the worse it got. It took me a long time to realize that I wasn't the problem. The way I had been operating—ignoring my limits, running on empty, pretending I could do everything without consequence—that was the problem.

I wish I could say there was some big turning point, a magical "aha" moment where I figured it all out. But the truth is, I had to slowly unlearn everything I thought I knew about productivity, success, and balance. I had to stop measuring my worth by how much I could get done in a day. I had to accept that I wasn't a machine—I was a human being with a finite amount of energy, and I needed to start treating myself like one.

This book is for anyone who has ever felt like I did. For the overachievers who are running on fumes. For the perfectionists who are exhausted from keeping it all together. For the people who look at their to-do lists and feel an overwhelming sense of dread.

I won't promise you a miracle fix, because there isn't one. What I *can* promise is a different way to approach life—one that makes space for rest, for boundaries, and for a version of success that doesn't come at the expense of your sanity.

Life, But Make It Manageable isn't about doing more. It's about doing *enough*. It's about making things *workable*. It's about learning to move through life with a little more ease and a lot less guilt.

If you've ever felt like you're carrying too much, you're not alone. Let's lighten the load together.

— Dr. Tia Warrick

Contents

CHAPTER

01

The Illusion of Control (And Why You Don't Have It)

SECTION 1: **The Grand Delusion— Thinking You Have Control**

The "Perfect Plan" Lie

Once upon a time, I thought I had my life under control. I was fresh out of grad school, armed with degrees, ambition, and a perfectly curated 5-year plan. I had the color-coded spreadsheets, the professional milestones lined up, and the delusional belief that if I worked hard enough, life would reward me with stability.

Then life said, "That's cute."

What actually happened? Within two years, I found myself juggling a whirlwind of responsibilities I never saw coming. My mother passed away. My career took unexpected turns. I moved into leadership roles that weren't even on my radar. And despite my best efforts to keep everything in a neat, logical sequence, reality laughed in my face and threw me plot twist after plot twist.

This is the moment when I realized: control is a scam.

We spend so much time planning, convinced that if we just prepare enough, we'll outsmart uncertainty. But the truth? Control is an illusion we create to make ourselves feel safe. And the moment we start thinking we've got it all figured out, life has a way of humbling us real quick.

There's nothing wrong with planning—I'm still a sucker for a well-organized to-do list—but the key is understanding that plans are just suggestions, not guarantees. The people who thrive aren't the ones who stick to their original blueprint no matter what. They're the ones who know how to pivot when the blueprint gets set on fire.

The Anxiety of Trying to Control Everything

I'll admit it: I used to be *that person*. The one who checked, double-checked, and triple-checked every detail. The one who sent confirmation emails for confirmation emails. The one who got an *actual headache* when someone said, "Let's just see how it goes."

Spoiler alert: that level of stress is not sustainable.

A few years ago, I was running a major research project. Every tiny detail had to be accounted for: lab schedules, data collection, equipment orders. I thought I had *everything* planned perfectly. Then one day, I got an email that turned my stomach inside out:

The shipment of critical lab supplies was delayed.

We weren't talking about a minor inconvenience. We were talking about a delay that could set the entire study back by months. I immediately spiraled into my usual cycle of overthinking: What if this ruined our timeline? What if we missed our deadlines? What if—heaven forbid—someone thought I was *incompetent*?

I spent hours calling suppliers, searching for last-minute solutions, basically trying to *force* a resolution into existence. And you know what happened? Absolutely nothing. The delay was out of my hands. The lab wasn't going to magically speed up. And all my stressing didn't make the shipment arrive any faster.

That was my lightbulb moment. I realized I had two choices:

1. Keep obsessing over something I couldn't change and make myself miserable.
2. Accept reality, shift the schedule, and move forward.

I chose Option #2. And guess what? The study still got done. The world did not end. No one burned my degrees in a ceremonial fire. And I saved myself from another unnecessary anxiety spiral.

Moral of the story: The more we cling to control, the more we suffer. Life will *always* throw us surprises. The question is whether we're going to let them break us, or whether we're going to roll with them.

The Universe's Sense of Humor

I used to believe that if I just worked hard, stayed focused, and made all the "right" choices, life would reward me accordingly. Then I realized that life is less of a meritocracy and more of a chaotic improv show.

Let's do a quick exercise. Think about the last time you made a big decision and thought, "This is it. I have it all figured out." Now think about how fast life completely obliterated that confidence.

> *You start a new job? Boom. Your boss resigns two weeks later.*
>
> *You book a dream vacation? Congrats. Your flight is canceled.*
>
> *You finally commit to going to the gym? Oh, look! A surprise back injury.*

Coincidence? Maybe. But I swear the universe has a twisted sense of humor.

For me, one of the biggest cosmic pranks came when I finally decided to take a well-deserved break. After working like a maniac for years—balancing academia, research, consulting, and life in general—I told myself, "Alright, Tia. It's time. You are going to rest."

I booked a solo trip. I scheduled zero meetings. I was ready to be that person who lounges in a hotel robe, sipping overpriced room service coffee, feeling *zen*.

Then, three days before departure, I got sick.

Not a cute, romantic kind of "stay-in-bed-and-watch-movies" sick. I'm talking *full-blown, can't-move, congestion-from-hell* sick.

The universe really said, *"You wanted a break? Here you go. You're not going anywhere."*

At first, I was pissed. How unfair! I finally tried to rest, and THIS is what I get?! But then I realized: this is exactly why we can't put happiness on hold for a "perfect" future moment.

We keep telling ourselves:

> *"I'll relax once things calm down."*

> *"I'll be happy once I achieve XYZ."*

> *"I'll enjoy life once everything is under control."*

But what if life never calms down? What if "control" is just a myth we keep chasing, hoping that one day, we'll finally feel safe?

Spoiler: that day never comes.

Instead of waiting for life to hand us perfect conditions, we have to learn how to enjoy the mess *as it is.* Because otherwise, we'll spend our whole lives waiting for a calm that never arrives.

The Takeaway: Let That Sh*t Go

If there's one thing I've learned, it's this: you don't need to control everything. You just need to trust that you'll handle whatever happens.

Plans will change.

People will disappoint you.

The unexpected will *always* happen.

But you? You're capable. You've made it through every unexpected moment before, and you'll make it through this one too.

So loosen your grip. Laugh when things go off-script. And remember: the most powerful person in the room isn't the one who has everything figured out. It's the one who knows how to pivot when the universe inevitably throws a curveball.

SECTION 2: **Life is a Game of Dodgeball (And You're Not Always Gonna Win)**

You remember dodgeball, right? That chaotic elementary school game where you either dodged for your life or got smacked in the face with a red rubber ball while your classmates cheered?

Yeah. That's life.

We can plan, prepare, and position ourselves perfectly, but at some point, a ball we *didn't see coming* is going to fly at our heads. The question isn't if you'll get hit. The question is: how fast can you recover?

The reality is, we don't get to control how many obstacles come flying our way. What we *can* control is how we respond—whether we let life knock us out of the game or whether we dust ourselves off and get back in the fight.

Expecting the Unexpected

Most of us walk around like life *owes* us predictability. We think if we do the right things, follow the "rules," and work hard, we'll be rewarded with smooth sailing.

But life doesn't give a damn about our expectations.

Case in point: My career. I spent years building my expertise in clinical research, thinking I had my trajectory mapped out. I had *plans*—big, structured, this-is-exactly-how-it's-going-to-go plans.

Then the world said, "Nah, try this instead."

At different points in my journey:

> I had to pivot from one role to another when opportunities shifted.

> I started a consulting business I never originally planned for.

I took on leadership roles that forced me to learn on the fly.

I wrote a whole damn book—even though I never saw myself as an "author."

None of this was on my original roadmap. And yet, every pivot brought me somewhere I was supposed to be.

This is why learning to expect the unexpected isn't just *helpful*—it's *necessary*. If you go through life assuming everything will unfold exactly as planned, you'll be in a *constant* state of disappointment. But if you train yourself to roll with the curveballs, nothing can truly shake you.

The Role of Adaptability: Why Winning is About Pivoting

Picture two people in a storm:

1. The first person stands firm, arms crossed, *refusing* to move because *this isn't how things were supposed to go!*
2. The second person grabs an umbrella, ducks under a bus stop, and figures out their next move.

Who's better off?

The ability to adapt—to pivot when necessary—is what separates people who thrive from people who just *survive*. The ones who stay stuck are the ones clinging to a *fantasy version* of how things were supposed to go. But the ones who learn to adapt? They turn obstacles into opportunities.

When I started working in public health, I *never* imagined I'd be where I am now—leading programs, running a consulting firm, mentoring future professionals. But every unexpected twist forced me to learn something new, to say *yes* to things I hadn't considered, to take risks even when I didn't feel ready.

And you know what? That's where the magic happens.

So when life *inevitably* throws a wrench in your plans, ask yourself:

Am I going to stand here and complain that this isn't what I expected?

Or am I going to pivot and figure out the next best step?

Adaptability isn't just about "going with the flow." It's about actively making the best out of whatever situation you land in. Because the truth is, some of the best opportunities in life come from situations that went *completely* off script.

How to Let Go (Without Giving Up)

A lot of people think that *letting go* means *giving up*. That's not true. Letting go just means acknowledging what you *can't* control and redirecting your energy toward what you *can*.

There's a massive difference between:

Quitting a job because you're scared and

Letting go of a job that's draining your soul and making space for something better.

Quitting on a dream because it got hard and

Letting go of the idea that it has to happen in a *specific* way.

Letting go is about *strategic surrender*. It's about recognizing that holding onto something that's *not working* is often more destructive than walking away.

When I was younger, I had this stubborn streak—this deep belief that if I just *tried harder*, things would eventually go the way I wanted. That if something wasn't working, I just had to push more.

Then I learned that sometimes, the best move is to stop forcing things.

When you find yourself fighting an uphill battle, ask yourself: Am I holding onto this because it's actually worth it, or am I just scared to let go?

Because sometimes, letting go isn't failing. Sometimes, it's just making room for something better.

Final Takeaway: Dodge, Pivot, Repeat

Life is a game of dodgeball. The balls *will* come flying. You *will* get hit sometimes. And no, you don't get to control every single thing that happens.

But what you *do* get to control is your response.

So when life throws something unexpected your way, remember:

▸ You can't control the storm, but you *can* control how you move through it.
▸ You don't have to cling to the way you *thought* things were supposed to go.
▸ The most powerful thing you can do is adapt, pivot, and keep going.

Because at the end of the day, winning isn't about dodging *every* ball. It's about making sure the ones that hit you don't take you out of the game.

SECTION 3: **The Myth of "Getting It Together"**

At some point, we were all sold the same lie: One day, we'll finally "get it together."

We imagine a future version of ourselves who wakes up at 5 AM, drinks green smoothies, never misses a deadline, and has life figured out. That version of us is thriving, unbothered, and effortlessly juggling work, relationships, and self-care like a pro.

That version of us? Doesn't exist.

Because the truth is, nobody actually has it together. Not your boss, not your favorite influencer, not the woman who makes six figures selling face serums. Everyone is winging it. Some people are just better at making it *look* like they're not.

Let's unpack this myth before it ruins your life.

Nobody Actually Knows What They're Doing

At every stage of life, we assume that other people have the answers—that adults, leaders, and successful people must have some *secret knowledge* that keeps everything running smoothly.

I hate to break it to you, but... they don't.

> **Doctors?** Yeah, they have medical training, but they're still making judgment calls.

> **CEOs?** They're making high-stakes decisions and hoping they don't tank the company.

> **Parents?** They're doing their best and hoping their kids don't end up in therapy over it.

There is no point at which you wake up and suddenly "arrive" at having life mastered. That's not how this works.

I used to assume that once I hit a certain level in my career, I'd feel different—more confident, more certain, more *together*. But guess what? The higher you climb, the more you realize nobody actually has a foolproof plan. Even the most accomplished people are still figuring it out as they go.

This is both terrifying and freeing. Because if nobody truly has it together, that means you don't have to either. You just have to keep going.

The Productivity Trap: Why "Doing More" Isn't the Answer

Somewhere along the way, we started equating *being productive* with *having our lives together*. We convinced ourselves that if we just work harder, optimize our time, and cram more into our schedules, we'll eventually hit that magical place where we feel completely in control.

Spoiler: That never happens.

The reality is, productivity can become a coping mechanism—a way to distract ourselves from the fact that life is inherently messy.

> We make to-do lists to feel like we're on top of things.

> We fill our schedules to avoid dealing with uncertainty.

> We chase accomplishments because we think they'll make us feel *enough*.

But productivity without purpose is just busyness. And busyness doesn't equal control—it just keeps you distracted.

I learned this the hard way. There was a time when I was juggling teaching, consulting, research, and a million side projects at once. My calendar was packed, my inbox was a war zone, and I was running on fumes. But instead of stopping to ask *why* I was doing all this, I just kept pushing.

Because if I kept moving, I wouldn't have to sit with the discomfort of not knowing what's next.

Sound familiar?

Here's the thing: If you're always in *go-go-go* mode but never feel satisfied, it's not because you need to do *more*. It's because you need to stop and reassess whether you're chasing the right things.

Having it together isn't about how much you do. It's about doing the right things for the right reasons.

When Control is Just Fear in a Fancy Outfit

Sometimes, our obsession with control isn't really about control at all. It's about fear.

Fear of failure.

Fear of looking stupid.

Fear of letting people down.

Fear of uncertainty.

So instead of admitting we're scared, we try to control everything around us. We micromanage our schedules. We overthink every decision. We stress about outcomes that haven't even happened yet.

But fear disguised as control is exhausting. It's like trying to hold back the ocean with your bare hands—it doesn't work, and you'll just end up tired and frustrated.

I used to be obsessed with *predicting* everything. I wanted certainty. I wanted guarantees. But life? Life doesn't work like that.

The moment I started accepting that uncertainty is a permanent feature of life—not a problem to be solved—things got *so much easier.*

The trick isn't to eliminate fear. That's impossible. The trick is to stop letting fear dictate your life.

You can be scared and still take action.

You can feel uncertain and still move forward.

You can acknowledge the unknown without trying to control it.

The people who succeed aren't the ones who *never* feel afraid. They're the ones who act despite the fear.

Final Takeaway: You Don't Need to "Get It Together"

If you take nothing else from this section, remember this:

▶ You will never reach a magical moment where you "have it all figured out."
▶ The most put-together people you know? They're just better at faking it.
▶ Productivity is great, but doing more isn't the same as living better.
▶ Control is just fear in disguise—let go of what you can't control and focus on what you can.

So stop chasing the myth of "having it together." Because the truth is, you're already doing better than you think.

SECTION 4: **What You Can Control (And What You Should Stop Trying To)**

By now, we've established that control is an illusion. Life is unpredictable, people are chaotic, and no amount of planning can protect you from the randomness of the universe.

But before you throw up your hands and start living like a reckless toddler with zero accountability, let's talk about what you can control. Because while you can't dictate every outcome, you do have power over certain things. The key is knowing the difference between what's in your hands and what you need to let go of.

Let's break it down.

Mastering the Art of "Letting That Sh*t Go"

There's a reason so many people feel *constantly* frustrated: they're trying to control things they were never meant to.

Here's a quick list of things you can't control, no matter how hard you try:

▶ Other people's opinions of you
▶ How someone chooses to behave
▶ Whether your boss acknowledges your hard work
▶ The past (sorry, but it's done)
▶ Unexpected life events

And yet, how much time do we spend obsessing over these things? How much energy do we waste worrying about whether someone likes us, whether an opportunity will work out, or whether things will go *exactly* as planned?

I'll be honest—I used to be a full-time overthinker. I wanted certainty. I wanted control. But all it did was drain me.

Then I had a game-changing realization:

If you can't control it, stressing about it is a waste of your damn time.

I know that sounds simple, but think about how much of your life is spent worrying about things that aren't even in your hands. Imagine what would happen if you took all that energy and redirected it to things you actually CAN influence.

Because while you can't control *everything*, you can control a lot more than you think.

Mindset, Actions, and Reactions: The Only Three Things You Control

If you're looking for a shortcut to peace of mind, here it is:

- ▶ Your Mindset – The way you choose to see a situation
- ▶ Your Actions – What you decide to do about it
- ▶ Your Reactions – How you respond to what happens

That's it. Those are the only three things you actually have power over.

Let's break them down:

1. Your Mindset (How You See Things)

Two people can experience the *exact* same situation but walk away with completely different perspectives.

- ▶ One person sees failure. The other sees a learning experience.
- ▶ One person sees rejection. The other sees redirection.
- ▶ One person sees obstacles. The other sees opportunities.

The difference? Mindset.

You don't always get to control what happens to you, but you do control the story you tell yourself about it. And the story you choose determines everything.

2. Your Actions (What You Do Next)

Life is going to happen whether you like it or not. The only question is: How are you going to respond?

> You didn't get the job—do you give up or apply for another?

> A relationship didn't work out—do you stay stuck in resentment or move forward?

> You feel lost—do you wait for clarity or take small steps anyway?

Every decision you make is a vote for the kind of person you want to be.

Even when life doesn't go your way, you always have a choice.

3. Your Reactions (How You Handle the Chaos)

Ever met someone who stays calm no matter what's happening? That's not because their life is easier than yours. It's because they've mastered their reactions.

> Someone says something rude? You control whether you engage.

> A situation is stressful? You control how much energy you give it.

> Things don't go your way? You control whether you spiral or strategize.

Emotional control isn't about being passive. It's about not letting external circumstances dictate your internal peace.

When you stop reacting to every little thing, you become unshakable.

Building a Life That Feels Good, Not Just One That Looks Good

A lot of people spend their entire lives chasing the idea of success—checking off boxes, collecting titles, making things *look* good on the outside—only to realize they're still miserable.

Why?

Because they were too busy trying to control external markers of success instead of focusing on how their life actually feels.

Let me put it bluntly: What's the point of looking successful if you feel like sh*t?

I had to learn this lesson myself. I spent years achieving things—degrees, career milestones, opportunities—but somewhere along the way, I forgot to actually enjoy the process.

It took me a while to understand that success isn't about how things look on paper. It's about how aligned your life feels to who you actually are.

So before you kill yourself trying to control every aspect of your life, ask yourself:

▸ Am I chasing this because I actually want it, or because I think I should want it?
▸ Am I measuring success by external validation, or by how I truly feel?
▸ Am I making decisions based on my own values, or based on fear?

Because at the end of the day, control is overrated—but clarity is everything.

Final Takeaway: Focus on What Actually Matters

Here's your new life mantra:

▶ If you can't control it, stop stressing about it.

▶ If you can control it, take action.

▶ It really is that simple.

The more you let go of things that aren't in your hands, the more energy you have for the things that are. And the more you focus on what you *can* control—your mindset, actions, and reactions—the more powerful you become.

So forget about the illusion of having everything together. Instead, focus on:

▶ Creating a life that feels good—not just one that looks impressive.

▶ Responding to challenges with clarity instead of panic.

▶ Trusting yourself to figure things out, even when the path isn't clear.

Because when you let go of the illusion of control, you gain something way better: real freedom.

CHAPTER

02

The Art of Selective Chaos

SECTION 1: **Not All Chaos is Bad— Why You Need a Little Mess**

Let's get one thing straight: a little chaos is necessary.

I know, I know. After spending an entire chapter talking about how control is an illusion, you might think the goal here is to eliminate chaos altogether. But here's the twist—if your life is too neat, too predictable, too perfectly planned, you're probably playing it too safe.

The truth is, controlled chaos is where the good stuff happens. Growth, creativity, adventure, risk-taking—none of it happens inside a perfectly structured, never-messy life. And if you're someone who has spent years trying to create a flawless, chaos-free existence, let me hit you with this reality check:

- Perfection is the enemy of progress.
- Trying to avoid all chaos will keep you stuck.
- The best moments of your life will probably happen in the middle of a mess.

Let's break it down.

Why Predictability is Overrated

If you're the type of person who craves routine, structure, and knowing *exactly* what's coming next, I get it. It feels safe. It feels *secure*. But here's the problem:

- Predictability doesn't challenge you.
- Predictability doesn't teach you anything new.
- Predictability doesn't open you up to new opportunities.

In fact, the more you try to control everything, the smaller your world becomes. You stop taking risks. You turn down new experiences. You avoid anything that might shake things up—even if it could lead to something amazing.

Let's be honest. Think about the moments in your life that truly shaped you:

> The time you took a job that was *way* outside your comfort zone.

> The time you moved to a new city and had to start fresh.

> The time you said "yes" to something that terrified you—and it changed everything.

None of those things happened because you played it safe.

They happened because you embraced a little bit of chaos.

The Fine Line Between Growth and Dysfunction

Now, before you start throwing all structure out the window, let's be clear: not all chaos is good chaos. There's a difference between embracing the mess of growth and living in a dumpster fire of dysfunction.

Here's how you can tell the difference:

Good chaos:

> Feels uncomfortable but exciting.

> Pushes you toward something meaningful.

> Challenges you to grow in ways you didn't expect.

> Forces you to be adaptable and resilient.

Bad chaos:

> Leaves you exhausted, drained, and constantly overwhelmed.

> Comes from ignoring red flags and hoping for the best.

Feels like you're running in circles instead of moving forward.

Pulls you into other people's drama and nonsense.

If you're constantly feeling burned out, stressed, or stuck in cycles that don't serve you, you're dealing with *destructive* chaos—not the kind that helps you grow. The trick isn't to eliminate chaos—it's to filter out the unnecessary mess and lean into the right kind of discomfort.

My Personal Chaos (And How It Changed Everything)

Let me tell you a little story about how chaos completely changed my life.

When I first started my consulting business, Lesous Consulting, I had *zero* clue what I was doing. I had built a solid career in research, I knew my industry, and I had plenty of experience—but running a business? That was a whole new level of chaos.

I had to figure out:

How to price my services *(because apparently, working for free isn't sustainable).*

How to handle contracts, invoices, and legal paperwork *(all the "fun" stuff).*

How to build relationships and pitch myself to clients *(without feeling like a total fraud).*

For someone who thrives on structure, this was terrifying. Nothing about it felt predictable or safe. There were no guarantees. No clear roadmap. Just me, taking risks and hoping for the best.

And you know what? That chaos was the best thing that ever happened to me.

Because in that discomfort, I grew.

Because in that uncertainty, I figured things out.

Because in that mess, I built something real.

If I had waited until I felt "ready," if I had refused to embrace the chaos of uncertainty, I never would have done it.

And that's the lesson: The best things in life come from taking risks before you feel 100% prepared.

How to Start Embracing the Right Kind of Chaos

So how do you lean into good chaos without letting your life spiral into dysfunction?

Here's a simple way to check yourself before making a move:

Ask yourself these questions before making a big decision:

Does this challenge me in a meaningful way? *(Growth is supposed to be uncomfortable, but it should still align with your bigger goals.)*

Am I scared because it's risky or because it's unfamiliar? *(Fear isn't always a bad thing—sometimes, it's just your brain resisting change.)*

Is this chaos pushing me forward or holding me back? *(There's a difference between an exciting challenge and a stressful, unnecessary mess.)*

Do I actually want this, or am I just afraid of missing out? *(Don't chase chaos for the sake of it—make sure it's leading somewhere you actually want to go.)*

If you answer yes to the first three questions, lean in. That's the kind of chaos that leads to something amazing.

If you're realizing this is just *unnecessary stress disguised as opportunity*, let it go.

Final Takeaway: Get Comfortable Being Uncomfortable

Here's the bottom line:

The best things in life happen outside your comfort zone.

If you wait for "perfect" conditions, you'll be waiting forever.

Controlled chaos is the secret ingredient to growth, success, and new opportunities.

So stop waiting for the perfect moment.

Stop trying to have everything figured out before you take the leap.

Stop running from every uncomfortable situation just because it feels messy.

Instead, ask yourself: What's the worst that could happen? And if the answer isn't "I will actually die," then maybe—just maybe—it's time to embrace the chaos and go for it.

SECTION 2: Pick Your Battles—Not Every Fire Needs Your Attention

One of the biggest lies we tell ourselves is that we have to fix everything.

Every problem at work.
Every issue in our family.
Every friend's emotional crisis.

And for what? To be the unofficial firefighter of everyone else's chaos? Absolutely not.

The truth is, not every fire is your fire. Not every problem needs your input, and not every crisis requires your intervention. Sometimes, the most powerful thing you can do is step back and let other people deal with their own mess.

Let's talk about how to stop running yourself ragged trying to fix everything and learn how to choose your battles wisely.

The Problem with Trying to Save Everything and Everyone

If you've ever found yourself exhausted from dealing with other people's problems, congratulations—you've fallen into the trap of over-responsibility.

This usually comes from one of three places:

You're a natural problem solver. You see an issue, and your first instinct is to fix it. Even when it's not your job.

You don't want to disappoint people. Saying no feels like letting people down, so you take on more than you should.

You mistake busyness for importance. If you're always involved, always needed, it makes you feel valuable—even if it's draining you.

The problem is that not every problem is yours to fix.

When you constantly insert yourself into fires that aren't yours, you waste time and energy on things that don't actually impact your life. You enable people who should be solving their own problems. You burn yourself out trying to save people who didn't ask to be saved.

The solution is getting clear on what actually deserves your energy.

The Three-Question Rule: Should You Get Involved?

Before jumping into a crisis, ask yourself these three critical questions.

Does this actually affect my life in a meaningful way? If it's not your issue, stay out of it.

Am I the right person to fix this? If someone else is responsible or more qualified, let them handle it.

Will this matter in a week, a month, or a year? If the answer is no, move on.

If your coworker is mad about something trivial, it's not your problem. If your sibling is dating a walking red flag, they'll figure it out eventually. If a stranger on social media doesn't like your opinion, block, delete, and carry on with your life.

Choosing your battles isn't about being passive. It's about protecting your peace.

Not Everyone Deserves Your Energy

Not everyone deserves access to your time and energy.

Some people will pull you into their chaos over and over again, and if you're not careful, you'll find yourself living in a constant state of stress over problems that aren't even yours.

There's the emotional dumper—this person constantly unloads their problems on you but never actually wants solutions. They just want someone to suffer with them.

Then there's the drama magnet—everything in their life is a crisis, and somehow, they always want you to fix it.

And of course, the energy leech—they take, take, take, and give nothing in return.

If you recognize any of these people in your life, ask yourself what you actually get from this relationship.

If the answer is exhaustion, frustration, or stress, it's time to set boundaries and pull back.

Not everyone's drama is your emergency. Let them deal with their own mess.

How to Step Back Without Feeling Guilty

If you're a natural helper, it can feel selfish to step back from people's problems. But here's the truth:

- ▸ You are not a bad person for protecting your energy.
- ▸ You do not owe anyone unlimited emotional labor.
- ▸ You cannot be everything for everyone—and you shouldn't try to be.

Here's how to step back without feeling like a bad person.

Practice the art of "That Sounds Hard." Next time someone dumps a problem on you, instead of immediately offering to help, try this:

"That sounds frustrating. I hope you figure it out."
"I know that's tough. What do you think you'll do about it?"
"That's a lot—I'm sure you'll handle it."

Watch what happens. Most of the time, people aren't looking for solutions. They just want to vent. And if they actually need help, they'll ask—which gives you the option to say yes or no.

Set boundaries with repeat offenders. If someone is constantly pulling you into their mess, it's time for a firm boundary.

"I care about you, but I can't be your go-to problem solver."

"I've given you advice before, and it sounds like this is something you need to work through on your own."

"I don't have the bandwidth for this right now, but I hope things get better."

At first, they might not like it. But that's not your problem. Your mental health is more important than their temporary frustration.

Give yourself permission to walk away. Sometimes, the best thing you can do is remove yourself from the situation entirely. If a person, job, or situation is consistently draining you, you don't need permission to leave.

Unfollow them.
Mute their texts.
Decline the invite.

Walk away without explaining yourself.

Not every battle is worth fighting. Some things are best left alone.

Final Takeaway: Stop Putting Out Fires That Aren't Yours

Not everything is your responsibility.

Not every problem needs your energy.

Not everyone deserves your emotional labor.

The less time you spend fixing things that aren't your job, the more time you have for what actually matters.

So next time someone tries to pull you into their storm, ask yourself:

Is this my problem?

Do I actually need to be involved?

Or can I step back and let them handle it?

Because real power doesn't come from controlling everything. It comes from knowing when to let go.

SECTION 3: **The Myth of "Balance" and Why It's Overrated**

People love to talk about work-life balance like it's some magical formula that, once achieved, makes life effortless. The idea is that if you just manage your time perfectly, juggle everything flawlessly, and set up the right routines, you'll feel completely in control.

That's not how this works.

Balance is a myth. If you're trying to keep everything at a perfect 50/50 split, you will constantly feel like you're failing. Life isn't about making sure every area of your life gets an equal amount of attention every day. It's about learning when to lean into certain things and when to let others take a back seat.

Some seasons of life require you to focus on your career more than your social life. Other times, your mental health needs to come before anything else. There are times when you have to drop the ball on purpose because something else is more important.

Trying to be great at everything, all the time, is a recipe for burnout. If you're overworking yourself to exhaustion, it's not because you haven't found balance—it's because you're trying to do too much.

Instead of aiming for perfect balance, get clear on what actually matters most at this moment. Let go of guilt for not being "perfect" in every area. Understand that different seasons require different priorities.

Balance isn't about trying to do everything. It's about being intentional with what you focus on and giving yourself permission to not feel bad about it.

The Time I Burned Myself Out Chasing Balance

I used to believe in the myth of balance. I thought if I just worked harder, planned better, and pushed through exhaustion, I'd reach some magical moment where I had it all together—thriving in my career, showing up perfectly for friends and family, keeping up with hobbies, working out, and still having time to relax.

That moment never came.

Instead, I ran myself into the ground trying to be *everything* at once.

At one point, I was juggling being a professor, running a consulting business, working on research, mentoring students, and speaking at conferences—all while trying to maintain a personal life. I told myself I could handle it. I convinced myself that if I just managed my time well enough, I'd be fine.

Then one day, I woke up and couldn't get out of bed.

I wasn't sick. I wasn't injured. I was just mentally and physically drained. My body had decided for me that I was done. It didn't matter how many planners I had or how organized my schedule was—my energy was gone.

That was the moment I realized balance wasn't real. I had been chasing something impossible. What I needed wasn't to "do everything better"—I needed to start letting go of things that weren't urgent, important, or necessary.

Why You Can't "Have It All" (At Least, Not All at Once)

People love to sell the idea that you can have it all. The career. The perfect social life. The dream relationship. The fit body. The hobbies. The personal growth. All of it, all at once, with zero stress.

That's a lie.

You can absolutely have different things at different times, but something will always require more of your energy. The key isn't trying to split yourself evenly between every aspect of life—it's being intentional about where you direct your time and attention based on what actually matters to you right now.

If your career is your focus this year, your personal life might take a backseat. If you're prioritizing your mental health, you might not be chasing promotions. If you're building a business, you probably won't have time for ten different hobbies.

Trying to do it all at once will leave you stretched too thin to enjoy any of it. The real goal isn't to balance everything equally—it's to make peace with the fact that different things will take priority at different times.

How I Learned to Let Some Things Go

After my burnout episode, I had to start dropping things on purpose.

I started asking myself, *What actually needs my attention right now? And what am I doing just because I feel like I "should" be doing it?*

I realized I didn't need to be at every meeting. I didn't need to accept every opportunity. I didn't need to be constantly available for everyone.

At first, I felt guilty. I had spent years believing that if I wasn't constantly grinding, I wasn't doing enough. But the more I let go of unnecessary stress, the more I realized:

▸ Nothing fell apart when I stopped overcommitting.
▸ People still respected me when I set boundaries.
▸ I finally had energy for the things that actually mattered.

The moment I stopped chasing balance, I started feeling in control again.

Why Some Things Will Always Be Unbalanced (And That's Okay)

There will always be one area of life that takes up more space than the others. Instead of resisting this, learn to embrace it. The more you fight the reality that some things will be neglected while others thrive, the more guilt and frustration you'll create for yourself.

The key is to be intentional about what gets your focus. If you know work is going to be your main priority for the next six months, make peace with the fact that you won't have time for as many social events. If your health is a focus, it's okay if you're not grinding at work at full speed.

It's not about doing everything perfectly—it's about knowing what matters most in the moment and being okay with the things that have to wait.

How to Drop the Ball on Purpose

One of the biggest mindset shifts you can make is learning to drop the ball strategically. Instead of feeling guilty about the things you can't get to, actively decide which things you're going to let slide.

Look at everything on your plate and ask yourself what actually needs your attention right now. Be honest about what can wait, what can be delegated, and what doesn't need to happen at all.

You don't have to be available for every social event. You don't have to say yes to every work request. You don't have to be running at full speed in every area of life just to prove that you have it together.

Giving yourself permission to let some things go for a while is one of the best things you can do for your mental health.

Final Takeaway: Focus on What Actually Matters Right Now

You don't need perfect balance. You need clarity on what actually deserves your time and energy at this moment. Some things will take a back seat, and that's okay. Different seasons of life will require different priorities. Instead of chasing balance, focus on being intentional with where you direct your effort and stop feeling guilty about the things that don't make the cut right now.

Stop trying to do it all. Start focusing on what actually matters.

SECTION 4: Learning to Say "No" Without Feeling Guilty

At some point in life, many of us were conditioned to believe that saying *no* is rude. That it makes us selfish. That if we really cared about people, we'd always be available.

Let me be clear: that is nonsense.

Saying no is one of the most powerful, necessary, and liberating skills you can develop. And yet, so many of us struggle with it—because we don't want to disappoint people, because we feel obligated, because we're afraid of being seen as difficult.

I used to be the queen of overcommitting. My schedule looked like a CVS receipt—long, overwhelming, and full of things I didn't actually need. Work commitments, social invites, last-minute favors, unpaid "opportunities" that promised exposure (*newsflash: exposure doesn't pay bills*). I said yes to things I didn't even want to do, just to avoid the awkward guilt of saying no.

Then one day, I hit my limit. My calendar was booked from sunrise to exhaustion, my inbox was a war zone, and I realized I was spending more time doing things for other people than I was for myself.

So I started practicing the art of *strategic refusal.* And let me tell you— saying no is a **life hack** no one talks about enough.

Why We Struggle to Say No (And Why That Needs to Stop)

If saying no makes you feel guilty, congratulations, you're a people-pleaser. Don't worry, so was I.

The guilt comes from this little voice in our heads that says:

▶ *"If I say no, they'll be disappointed."*

▶ *"If I say no, they'll think I'm selfish."*

▶ *"If I say no, I might miss out on something important."*

Here's the truth: disappointing people is inevitable. You will never be able to meet everyone's expectations, and honestly, it's not your job to.

And let's talk about the word "selfish." Somewhere along the way, "selfish" became this all-encompassing insult that made us feel like garbage for putting our own well-being first. But protecting your time and energy is not selfish—it's survival.

How I Started Saying No (Without the Over-Explaining Nonsense)

One of the biggest mistakes people make when saying no is over-explaining.

I used to do this all the time. If someone invited me to an event I didn't want to go to, I'd write them an entire essay about why I couldn't make it, complete with excessive justifications and fake regret.

"I would *love* to, but I have a lot of work, and I already made plans to do some self-care, and I have to wake up early tomorrow, and also my plants need watering, so I can't, but maybe next time!!"

Unnecessary.

A simple "I can't make it, but I hope you have fun!" is all that's needed.

Here's the golden rule of saying no: you do not owe anyone a detailed explanation for protecting your time.

Let's look at some upgraded ways to say no without the guilt trip:

"I won't be able to, but thanks for thinking of me."

"That doesn't fit into my schedule right now."

"I can't commit to that, but I appreciate the offer."

"I'm focusing on other priorities at the moment."

"No, but I wish you the best with it!"

Short. Clear. No unnecessary guilt.

When Saying No Feels Uncomfortable— Say It Anyway

I won't lie—if you're used to being a yes-person, saying no will feel uncomfortable at first.

The first few times I started setting boundaries, I expected people to be mad. I braced myself for the guilt trip, the silent treatment, the passive-aggressive "I guess I just won't ask you for anything anymore" responses.

And you know what happened?

Most people just said "Okay, no problem."

The world didn't end. I didn't lose my friendships. People just... moved on.

The ones who *did* get weird about it? They were the same ones who had been benefiting from my lack of boundaries for years. And that was my wake-up call: the only people who get mad when you set boundaries are the ones who were taking advantage of you having none.

Saying no isn't about being mean. It's about choosing yourself first.

The Life-Changing Benefits of Saying No More Often

Once I started saying no, a funny thing happened—I had so much more time. Time for actual priorities. Time for rest. Time for things that mattered to *me*, not just to everyone else.

By cutting out the unnecessary yeses, I started:

▶ Sleeping better because I wasn't constantly overbooked.

▶ Enjoying my work more because I wasn't taking on projects I hated.

▶ Strengthening my relationships because I was showing up *fully* for the things I actually wanted to be part of.

Saying no gave me my life back.

If you're feeling stretched too thin, overworked, and constantly overwhelmed, take a hard look at where your time is going. How many things on your plate are there because you were afraid to say no?

How to Start Saying No (Without Feeling Like a Jerk)

If you're ready to start saying no, but the words still feel stuck in your throat, here's your action plan:

1. Start Small
If saying no feels terrifying, practice with low-stakes situations. Decline a minor request, turn down a casual invite, or politely refuse an obligation that doesn't serve you.

2. Remind Yourself That No is a Complete Sentence
You don't need an excuse. You don't need a novel-length explanation. A simple "I can't" is enough.

3. Expect Some Resistance
People who are used to you always saying yes might be surprised at first. That's fine. Their expectations don't dictate your boundaries.

4. Check Your Calendar Before Committing

Instead of automatically saying yes, buy yourself time. "Let me check my schedule and get back to you" gives you space to decide if you actually want to do something.

5. Own Your No With Confidence

The more comfortable you become saying no, the easier it gets. Over time, you'll realize that saying no doesn't make people mad—it just makes room for the things that actually matter.

Final Takeaway: Saying No is Self-Care, Not Selfishness

No, you are not obligated to do things just because someone asked.
No, you do not have to explain yourself every time you say no.
No, you don't have to make yourself available for everyone else's needs at the expense of your own.

Start saying no more often, and watch how much lighter your life becomes.

CHAPTER

03

Burnout Ain't a Badge of Honor

SECTION 1: **The Burnout Epidemic— Why We're All Tired as Hell**

I don't remember the exact moment I burned out.

There was no dramatic collapse. No rock-bottom epiphany. No scene where I sobbed in the shower and realized I needed to change my life. It wasn't a single moment at all.

It was a slow, quiet unraveling.

- ▸ It was waking up after eight hours of sleep and still feeling like I hadn't rested in years.
- ▸ It was forgetting why I walked into a room—so many times that I started feeling like I was losing my mind.
- ▸ It was feeling *resentment*—deep, ugly resentment—toward things I used to love.
- ▸ It was hearing people say, *"You're doing amazing!"* and wondering how the hell they didn't see that I was running on fumes.

Burnout is not exhaustion. Exhaustion can be cured with sleep. Burnout is something deeper, something that sinks into your bones. A quiet kind of misery that no amount of caffeine, productivity hacks, or "self-care Sundays" can fix.

And yet, for the longest time, I refused to call it burnout. Because that would mean admitting I was breaking.

I didn't want to break. I wanted to be strong.

So I did what we all do—I kept going.

I worked through the exhaustion. I smiled through the resentment. I pushed through every "off" feeling, telling myself I'd feel better *once things calmed down.*

But things never calmed down.

Because burnout is not something you outwork. And the longer you ignore it, the more it eats you alive.

The Lies We Tell Ourselves About Burnout

If I had to pick the single most destructive thought that kept me stuck in burnout, it would be this:

"If I just push through a little longer, it'll get better."

It won't.

Burnout is not a storm that passes on its own. It doesn't fade with time. It doesn't heal itself when you hit your next goal, your next milestone, your next *breakthrough*.

But we tell ourselves these lies because the alternative—stopping, reassessing, doing something different—feels impossible.

So instead, we say things like:

"It's just a busy season." (Except the "season" never ends.)
"I'll slow down once I finish this project." (Then another one takes its place.)
"I'm just tired—I'll take a break next weekend." (But next weekend comes, and you don't.)

And the worst one of all:

"I don't have a choice."

Because that's what burnout does. It makes you believe that rest is not an option. That if you stop, everything will fall apart. That the only way out is through—even when "through" is killing you.

The Slow Death of Passion and Joy

The scariest thing about burnout is not the exhaustion.

It's the way it steals the things that make life feel worth living.

I used to love my work. I loved writing, teaching, mentoring, creating. These things used to light me up. They made me feel alive.

And then one day, they didn't.

One day, the things I loved became just another set of tasks to complete. Just another checkbox on an endless list.

I didn't even notice it at first. It's not like you wake up one morning and suddenly *hate* everything. It's more like a slow leak—barely noticeable at first, until one day you realize you're completely empty.

And what do you do when the thing that once made you feel alive now just makes you feel tired?

If you're like me, you tell yourself to *be grateful.*

"You're lucky to be doing this work."
"Other people would kill for these opportunities."
"You're being ungrateful—suck it up and keep going."

But gratitude does not cure burnout.

Because burnout is not about hating what you do. It's about losing yourself in the process of doing it.

The Moment I Realized I Was Lost

It wasn't the exhaustion that scared me.

It wasn't the brain fog, or the constant feeling of "I can't keep up."

It was the day I looked at my own life—the life I had built, the life I had *wanted*—and thought:

"I don't want to be here anymore."

Not in a *life-ending* way. In a *"I want to disappear for a while" kind of way.*

I fantasized about quitting everything. Not because I hated it, but because I was too tired to keep doing it. I dreamed about packing a bag, getting on a plane, and running somewhere no one could reach me.

I wanted to disappear, not because I didn't love my life, but because I didn't recognize myself in it anymore.

And that's when I knew.

Burnout hadn't just drained my energy. It had stolen me.

What Burnout Really Does to You

Burnout makes you a stranger in your own life.

It turns everything you once cared about into obligations.
It makes rest feel unearned.
It makes you feel guilty for not doing more, even when you're already drowning.

And worst of all?

It makes you believe that this is just how life is supposed to feel.

It convinces you that everyone else is just *better* at handling it. That you're the weak one. That you need to be *tougher, more disciplined, more resilient.*

But burnout is not a sign that you're weak.

Burnout is a sign that you've been strong for too long.

Final Takeaway: You Are Not Supposed to Feel Like This

Let me say this loud enough for the people in the back:

You are not supposed to feel like this.

You are not supposed to be this tired all the time.
You are not supposed to feel guilty for resting.
You are not supposed to survive your life instead of living it.

And if you are waiting for permission to stop—this is it.

Because if you don't stop now, burnout will do what burnout always does:

It will take everything from you until there's nothing left.

And you deserve better than that.

SECTION 2: **The Lies We Tell Ourselves About Rest**

I used to think rest was something you *earned.*

That if I just worked hard enough, checked off enough boxes, did *enough*, then I'd finally be allowed to slow down.

But rest is not a reward.

Rest is maintenance.

You don't wait until your car's engine explodes before getting an oil change. You don't wait until your phone is completely dead before charging it. But somehow, when it comes to ourselves, we believe we have to earn the right to take care of ourselves.

And that belief? It's exactly why so many of us are walking around one bad day away from total collapse.

The Myth of "Deserved" Rest

I used to measure whether or not I was allowed to rest by how much I had "accomplished" that day.

Did I finish my entire to-do list?
Did I get enough done?
Did I *earn* the right to stop?

But here's the problem: the finish line always moved.

No matter how much I did, there was always more. Another email to send. Another task to complete. Another reason to keep going.

And that's when I realized—if you have to earn rest, you will never be allowed to take it.

Because the work will never be done.

Your inbox will never be empty.
Your to-do list will never be complete.
There will always be something pulling at your time, your energy, your attention.

And if you don't set a boundary, the world will never set one for you.

The "Lazy" Fear and Why We're Terrified of Doing Nothing

One of the hardest things about learning to rest? The nagging voice in the back of your head whispering, *"You should be doing something."*

Because we've been trained to believe that doing nothing is failure.

We admire the grind. We celebrate the people who are always "on." We have entire industries built around hustle culture, side hustles, and monetizing every hobby—because why would you rest when you could be turning your free time into *more productivity?*

And so we learn to feel guilty for resting.

Guilty for taking a break when other people are still working.
Guilty for closing our laptops while someone else is still answering emails.
Guilty for watching TV when we could be "bettering ourselves."

We don't rest. We "strategically recharge" so we can work more efficiently.

We don't take time off. We "invest in self-care" so we can be more productive.

Even our rest is infected with the expectation of output.

And that is why we are all so damn exhausted.

Fake Rest vs. Real Rest: Why You're Still Tired

Here's the thing: a lot of us think we're resting, but we're not.

We're just switching to a different kind of output.

> Lying in bed but scrolling through emails? Not rest.

> Taking a break but still feeling guilty? Not rest.

> Binge-watching a show but mentally tallying up tomorrow's to-do list? Not rest.

Real rest is not just the absence of work.

Real rest is the absence of guilt.

It's allowing yourself to exist without the pressure to produce something.

And for those of us who have spent years tying our worth to our productivity? That kind of rest feels like failure.

The First Time I Took a Guilt-Free Break (And Almost Had a Panic Attack About It)

I remember the first time I tried to take a *real* break—no work, no emails, no mental checklists. Just rest.

It was a random Sunday. I had nothing urgent to do. No looming deadlines. No immediate crises.

I told myself: Today, I'm just going to relax.

And I lasted about six minutes before my brain went into full panic mode.

"You're wasting time."
"You should at least be doing something productive."
"There are a million things you could be catching up on right now."

It was so uncomfortable that I almost got up and started working just to make the anxiety stop.

That's when I realized: I wasn't just bad at resting. I was afraid of it.

Afraid that if I slowed down, I'd fall behind.
Afraid that if I stopped, I wouldn't be able to start again.
Afraid that if I wasn't constantly *doing*, then who even was I?

Because when you spend your whole life measuring your worth by what you produce, the idea of stopping feels like erasing yourself.

The Hardest Lesson About Rest: You Have to Take It Before You "Need" It

Burnout doesn't show up overnight. It builds in layers, quietly, slowly.

A little fatigue here. A little resentment there.
A few skipped meals. A few too many late nights.
A creeping sense of exhaustion that starts to feel normal.

Until one day, you wake up and you have nothing left to give.

And by the time you reach that point, rest isn't enough anymore.

Because real recovery doesn't come from *crash-landing* into rest when you're already broken.

It comes from building it into your life before burnout forces you to.

You do not have to be falling apart to justify slowing down.
You do not have to be on the verge of collapse to deserve rest.
You do not have to earn your right to exist without working.

You can just... rest. Because you're human. Because you deserve it. Because it's your life, and you do not have to spend it exhausted.

Final Takeaway: If You Don't Choose Rest, Burnout Will Choose It for You

If you're waiting for permission to rest, here it is.

Not later. Not when you finish your next project. Now.

Because if you don't choose rest, burnout will force it upon you. And when that happens, it won't be on your terms.

It won't be a relaxing weekend or a day off. It'll be a full-body shutdown. A mental breakdown. A crash that takes months or years to recover from.

Don't wait for that.

Because here's the truth: The world will keep spinning without you. The work will still be there when you get back. But you?

You only get one you.

And you cannot afford to lose yourself just because you were afraid to sit still.

SECTION 3: **How to Spot Burnout Before It Wrecks You**

Burnout doesn't show up at your door like an uninvited guest, loudly announcing its arrival. It doesn't kick down the door and scream, "Hey! You're working yourself into the ground! You should stop now!"

No.

Burnout is quiet. It's a slow leak, a barely noticeable unraveling. It doesn't show up all at once—it creeps. It seeps. It whispers.

And by the time you finally notice it? It's already wrapped itself around you like a weighted blanket soaked in concrete.

The trick isn't learning how to *recover* from burnout. It's learning how to spot it before it steals you.

The Lies We Tell Ourselves to Ignore Burnout

The first stage of burnout isn't exhaustion. It's denial.

You tell yourself you're just in a "busy season." That things will calm down soon. That once you get through this next project, this next deadline, this next obligation—then you'll rest.

But you don't.

Because there's always another thing waiting. And before you know it, you're six months deep into an "intense season" that has somehow become your entire life.

I remember the first time someone told me I looked tired. I shrugged it off. *I'm fine. Just a little busy.*

Then another person said it. And another.

Until one day, I looked at my own face in the mirror and saw it for myself.

Not just tired. Worn. Hollow. Edges frayed like an old, over washed sweater.

But still, I told myself I was fine.

Because what was the alternative? Slowing down? Letting something go? Admitting I wasn't superhuman?

Nope. Absolutely not. Instead, I doubled down.

Worked harder. Slept less. Ignored every red flag my body was frantically waving.

And that's how burnout wins.

Not by showing up overnight. But by convincing you to ignore it until it's too late.

The Warning Signs You Keep Ignoring

So, how do you know burnout is creeping in? Before it wrecks you?

Here's what I wish someone had told me before I let it get too far:

1. You wake up tired—even when you get enough sleep.
Not the kind of tired that a good night's rest can fix. The kind of tired that sits in your bones. The kind of tired that no amount of coffee, naps, or extra hours in bed can erase.

2. You stop caring about things you used to love.
Burnout doesn't just drain your energy—it drains your joy.
The things that used to excite you now feel like chores. Hobbies, relationships, even basic human interaction starts feeling like work.

3. You are irrationally irritated all the time.
Burnout turns tiny inconveniences into full-blown catastrophes.
A slow internet connection? Rage-inducing.

A mildly annoying email? Personal attack.
Someone chewing too loudly? Grounds for exile.

It's not that people are more annoying—it's that your nervous system is fried.

4. Your memory starts glitching.
You walk into a room and forget why.
You stare at an email you just wrote and it looks like nonsense.
You start dropping the ball on things you *never* used to forget.

Your brain is like an overloaded browser—too many tabs open, everything slowing down, and eventually, the whole system crashes.

5. You fantasize about running away.
And I don't mean a cute vacation. I mean full-blown, pack-a-bag-and-vanish-into-the-wilderness type of escape.
Not because you hate your life. But because the thought of continuing at this pace feels impossible.

If you recognize yourself in any of these, this is your sign.

Not to push through. To stop.

Because burnout doesn't get better by *ignoring* it.

How Burnout Feels in Real Life

The worst part of burnout is that it makes everything feel impossible.

Simple things. Easy things. Things that used to take zero effort now feel like climbing Everest with bricks in your backpack.

For me, it wasn't just work that became unbearable. It was everything.

Making a doctor's appointment? Too much effort.
Replying to a text? Couldn't do it.

Cooking an actual meal instead of eating cereal straight from the box? *Absolutely not.*

And here's what makes burnout so insidious: It convinces you that this is just who you are now.

That the exhaustion, the numbness, the lack of motivation—it's *not* a temporary problem. It's just... *you.*

And that is the most dangerous lie burnout will ever tell you.

Because this is not you. This is burnout talking.

And you do not have to live like this.

The Crash: When Your Body Decides It's Done

Here's what people don't tell you:

If you don't listen to burnout when it whispers, it will eventually scream.

And by then? You don't get to negotiate.

Your body will shut down *for* you.
Your brain will refuse to function.
Your motivation will be completely gone.

And suddenly, you're no longer *choosing* whether to keep going or take a break—your body is making the choice for you.

I learned this the hard way.

I ignored every sign. Every red flag. Every moment where my body said, "Please, just slow down."

And then one day, I just... stopped working.

Not just physically—mentally. Emotionally. I sat at my desk, looked at my laptop, and I *couldn't do it anymore.*

Not "I didn't want to."
Not "I needed a break."
I literally. Could. Not.
I had burned through every reserve. There was nothing left.

And that's when I realized: I had been running on empty for so long that I had forgotten what it felt like to be full.

Final Takeaway: Burnout Will Steal You If You Let It

If you're reading this and thinking, *"Damn, this sounds familiar,"* then please—take this as your sign.

Because burnout will take everything from you if you let it.

It will steal your energy.
Your joy.
Your ability to feel like yourself.

And the longer you ignore it, the harder it will be to find your way back.

You do not have to keep going at this pace.
You do not have to run yourself into the ground.
You do not have to prove anything to anyone at the cost of your own well-being.

This is your permission to stop.

Not later. Now.

Because burnout doesn't ask permission.
It doesn't wait until it's "convenient."
It doesn't give you a polite warning before it destroys you.

It just takes.
Unless you stop it first.

SECTION 4: **Breaking the Cycle—How to Stop Living on the Edge of Burnout**

Burnout is a thief. It sneaks in, rearranges your priorities, and convinces you that your exhaustion is just *commitment*. That your declining health is just *the price of success*. That your inability to feel excitement is just *adulthood*.

It takes and takes and takes—your energy, your joy, your ability to give a damn.

And what do we do?

We let it.

We justify it. We tell ourselves that we're just "pushing through a busy season." That once we finish *this* project, hit *this* milestone, survive *this* week—then we'll slow down.

Except we never do.

Because the world doesn't slow down. And if you don't break the cycle yourself, burnout will keep you running until there's nothing left of you but the running.

Why We Don't Stop (Even When We Know We Should)

If burnout were just about being tired, we'd fix it with sleep.

But it's deeper than that.
Burnout is about fear.

- ▶ Fear that if we stop, we'll fall behind.
- ▶ Fear that if we rest, we'll be seen as lazy.
- ▶ Fear that if we stop holding everything together, our lives will collapse under the weight of everything we've been carrying.

So we keep going. Because stopping feels like a bigger risk than exhaustion.

And this is what burnout wants you to believe—that you *can't* stop. That you *shouldn't* stop. That stopping is failure.

It's not.

It's survival.

Because if you don't stop on purpose, burnout will stop you *by force.* And when that happens, it won't be a long weekend and a nap that fixes it. It'll be months—maybe years—of trying to find yourself again.

How to Stop Before Burnout Stops You

You don't need a life overhaul. You don't need to quit your job, move to the mountains, and start selling homemade candles (unless you *want* to).

But you do need to change how you live inside your own life.

Here's how:

1. Unlearn the Idea That Your Worth Is in Your Work

You are not what you produce.

Read that again.

The world has tricked us into believing that our value is tied to our output. That if we're not constantly achieving, then we're falling behind. That if we're not *doing something productive,* then we're *wasting time.*

This is a lie.

Your worth does not change whether you answer 100 emails or none. Whether you wake up at 5 AM to journal and meditate or sleep until noon. Whether you say yes to every opportunity or let some pass you by.

Your worth just is. It's not something you earn. It's something you *own.*

2. Break Up with Busyness

Some of us are addicted to being needed.

We wear "busy" like a status symbol. We complain about our packed schedules while secretly feeling proud of them. Because in a world that rewards burnout disguised as ambition, the worst thing you can be is *idle.*

But if you are always on, if you are always available, if you are always needed—who is taking care of you?

Busyness is not the same thing as importance.

Stop confusing exhaustion with meaning.

3. Stop Using Rest as a Reward

The reason so many of us don't rest is because we've turned it into a finish line we never reach.

We say, *"I'll rest once I finish this."*

Then we finish. And another thing takes its place. And another. And another.

And suddenly, rest is always just out of reach.

But rest is not something you earn.

Rest is maintenance. It's oxygen. It's a non-negotiable.

You don't wait until you're starving to eat. You don't wait until your car is totaled to get a tune-up. You don't wait until your lungs give out to take a breath.

So stop waiting until you crash to take care of yourself.

4. Learn to Say "No" Without an Essay

If burnout had a best friend, it would be overcommitment.

Somewhere along the way, we became terrified of disappointing people. We started believing that "no" needed to come with an explanation, a justification, a guilt-ridden apology.

It doesn't.

- ▶ "I can't take that on right now."
- ▶ "That doesn't fit into my schedule."
- ▶ "I won't be able to, but thanks for asking."

No overexplaining. No "I wish I could." No making up fake excuses.

The world will not end if you disappoint someone. But you might if you don't start choosing yourself.

SECTION 5: **Remember That Rest Isn't Just About Stopping—It's About Rebuilding**

Burnout recovery isn't just about doing less.

It's about making space for more of what fills you.

Ask yourself:

- ▶ What's the last thing you did that made you feel alive?
- ▶ What's something you used to love but don't make time for anymore?
- ▶ What does joy look like when it's not attached to productivity?

Burnout takes away your ability to feel anything. Recovery is about feeling everything again.

The Hardest Part of Recovery: Believing You Deserve It

The biggest barrier to stopping burnout isn't time. It's belief.

The belief that you can rest without feeling guilty.
The belief that you can slow down without losing momentum.
The belief that you don't have to destroy yourself to matter.

Because the world will never give you permission to stop.
There will always be something else to do.
There will always be another reason to keep going.

Which means you have to be the one to choose.

To stop before burnout stops you.
To rest before your body forces you to.
To choose yourself—not when everything is falling apart, but before it ever gets to that point.

Final Takeaway: You Don't Need to Earn the Right to Rest

At the end of your life, no one is going to stand up at your funeral and list your achievements.

No one is going to say, "Wow, she answered emails at midnight. She was always exhausted but never said no to anything. She was a master of burnout."

That is not the legacy you are meant to leave.

You are not here to work yourself to death.
You are not here to spend every waking moment proving your worth.
You are not here to be useful at the expense of being whole.

You are here to live.

And that means learning to rest before burnout makes the choice for you.

CHAPTER

04

Boundaries—The Ultimate Life Hack

If burnout is the disease, boundaries are the cure.

Not self-care. Not another planner. Not a *better* time management system. Boundaries.

But let's be honest—most of us suck at them.

We say yes when we mean no. We over-explain when we don't have to. We feel guilty for protecting our time, our energy, and our sanity.

And then we wonder why we're exhausted, resentful, and one mildly inconvenient email away from quitting everything to go live in the woods.

Boundaries are not just a cute Instagram quote about *"protecting your peace."* They are the difference between living your life and letting it be consumed by everyone else's demands.

This chapter is about how to actually set them—and stick to them—without guilt, without apology, and without losing your damn mind.

Let's break it down into four sections.

SECTION 1: Why You Struggle with Boundaries (And How to Fix It)

Let's get one thing straight: If you struggle with boundaries, it's not because you're too nice.

It's because, at some point, you were taught that other people's needs matter more than your own.

Maybe you grew up in a house where saying no wasn't an option. Where keeping the peace meant sacrificing your own. Where love felt conditional, tied to how much you could give, how much you could do, how much of yourself you were willing to hand over.

Or maybe the world just wore you down.

You learned that the best way to be liked is to be *accommodating*.

You learned that the easiest way to avoid conflict is to say *yes* when you mean *no*.

You learned that if you want to keep people in your life, you better not be difficult.

So you became the person who...

> ▶ Answers the phone even when you don't feel like talking.
> ▶ Picks up extra work because "no one else will do it."
> ▶ Says "sure" when every part of you is screaming "please, God, no."

And over time, this became who you are.

The reliable one.
The easygoing one.
The one who's always *there*—even when you're drowning.

The Cost of Being "The One Everyone Can Count On"

Here's the thing about being the person everyone relies on:

It's exhausting.

Because the more available you are, the more people expect you to be.
The more you give, the less people think to ask if you even *want* to.
The more you show up for others, the easier it becomes for them to forget to show up for you.

And at first, it feels good. You like being needed. You like being useful.
But eventually, it doesn't feel like kindness anymore.

It feels like obligation.

Like you don't have a choice.
Like people only keep you around because of what you can do for them.

Like if you stopped giving, if you stopped saying yes, if you stopped being so available—they might leave.

And maybe that's the real fear.

Not that you'll disappoint people.
Not that someone will call you selfish.
But that if you stop overextending yourself, you'll find out who's really here for you—and who was just here for what you could offer.

Why Boundaries Feel So Damn Hard to Set

The reason you don't set boundaries isn't because you *can't*.

It's because setting them feels dangerous.
Not physically, maybe. But emotionally. Socially.
Because boundaries change relationships.

And change is scary.

> You worry people will be disappointed.

> You worry they'll take it personally.

> You worry they'll leave.

> You worry that saying no means you're rejecting them—not just the request, but *them as a person.*

And if you're someone who has spent your whole life keeping people happy at your own expense, then the thought of making someone uncomfortable—even just a little—is terrifying.

So you keep saying yes. You keep showing up. You keep prioritizing other people's comfort over your own well-being.

Until one day, you realize you're not even in control of your own life anymore.

You've given it away—piece by piece, favor by favor, "sure" by "sure."

And you are so, so tired.

What No One Tells You About Setting Boundaries

Here's the truth no one tells you about setting boundaries:

It will feel bad at first.

Not because it's wrong. But because you're not used to it.

When you start saying no, you will feel selfish.
When you start pulling back, you will feel like a bad friend, a bad daughter, a bad person.
When people react negatively, you will feel guilty.

Because for the first time, you are doing something for yourself.

And that? That is unfamiliar territory.

But listen to me—this is the part where most people give up.

They set a boundary. Someone gets upset. The guilt creeps in. And they backtrack.

> *"Okay, fine, I'll help."*

> *"Never mind, I can still make it."*

> *"Forget what I said, it's not a big deal."*

And just like that, the boundary crumbles.

But here's what you need to know:

Discomfort is part of the process.
The first time you set a boundary, it will feel wrong.
The second time, it will feel slightly less wrong.

The third time, it will start to feel normal.
And eventually, it will feel like freedom.

The Turning Point: When You Realize Your Energy is Yours to Protect

There is a moment that happens when you finally commit to boundaries.

A moment when you say no—and instead of explaining, instead of softening, instead of rushing to make the other person feel better, you just let it be.

And when they react? When they guilt-trip you? When they try to pull you back into the role you've always played?

You don't bend.
You don't negotiate.
You don't shrink yourself to make them comfortable.

And suddenly, you realize: nothing bad happens.

You're still standing.
You're still breathing.
And the world? It didn't end.

That's when it clicks.

That you do not exist to be available at all times.
That your time and energy are yours to protect.
That you don't have to prove your worth by how much you endure.

Final Takeaway: You Can Set Boundaries and Still Be Loved

Let me tell you something I wish someone had told me sooner:

The right people? The ones who truly love and respect you?

They will not leave just because you have boundaries.

They will not make you feel guilty for needing space.
They will not take your "no" as rejection.
They will not demand that you exhaust yourself for their comfort.

Because real love—real, deep, genuine love—does not require self-sacrifice.

And anyone who makes you feel like you have to choose between your peace and their approval?

That is someone you should never have to prove yourself to in the first place.

SECTION 2: **How to Set Boundaries Without Feeling Like an Asshole**

The first time you set a real boundary, it will feel wrong.

Not because it is. But because you've spent your entire life being conditioned to believe that your needs should come last.

So the moment you start saying, *"No, I can't do that,"* or *"I need space,"* or *"I'm not available for that,"*—your brain freaks out.

It panics. It tells you:

> *"You're being selfish."*

> *"You're making things harder for everyone else."*

> *"They're going to be mad at you."*

And for a second, you consider backtracking. Saying yes even though you don't want to. Smoothing it over so no one's uncomfortable.

Because that's what you've always done.

But here's what you need to understand:

Having boundaries does not make you mean. It makes you clear.

And clarity? Clarity is what protects you from becoming a walking doormat.

The Hardest Part of Setting Boundaries: The Guilt

Let's get one thing straight—the guilt isn't real.

It feels real. It feels overwhelming. But it's just a symptom of being untrained in protecting your own space.

Guilt is what happens when a people-pleaser starts choosing themselves. Guilt is what happens when someone who's spent their life over-giving finally stops.

Guilt is what happens when you realize you don't owe everyone unlimited access to you.

But guilt is not a reason to fold.

Because guess what? The people who genuinely care about you won't be upset when you set a boundary.

And the people who do get mad? They were benefiting from your lack of one.

The No-Bullsh*t Guide to Setting Boundaries (And Actually Sticking to Them)

If you want to set boundaries without guilt, without drama, and without backtracking, here's the formula:

1. Say It Short, Say It Straight

Weak boundaries sound like:

> *"I mean, I guess I could, but I was really hoping to rest..."*
> *"I'd rather not, but if you really need me to, I guess I could try..."*
> *"I have a lot going on, but I'll see if I can squeeze it in..."*

That is not a boundary. That is an invitation to be convinced.

Strong boundaries sound like:

> "I'm not available for that."
> "That doesn't work for me."
> "I can't commit to that right now."

No explanations. No softening. No giving people room to argue their way back into your time.

2. Stop Apologizing for Having Needs

You do not have to say, "I'm so sorry, but I can't."

You do not have to soften your boundary so the other person doesn't feel bad.

You are allowed to take up space without apologizing for it.

Instead of:
"I hate to say no, but..." → Just say no.
"I really wish I could, but..." → If you wished you could, you would.
"I feel bad, but I just can't..." → Why do you feel bad for taking care of yourself?

Own it. No guilt. No apology.

3. Don't Give an Opening for Negotiation

Some people will test your boundaries to see if you really mean them.

> *"Are you sure? It'll only take a few minutes!"*
> *"But you're so good at this, it'd be so helpful!"*
> *"I know you're busy, but can you just squeeze this in?"*

And this is where a lot of people cave.

Because they don't want to sound difficult.
Because they feel like they *should* help.
Because they worry about disappointing people.

But the second you say, *"Well... I guess I could try,"* you just lost your boundary.

If someone pushes, repeat your boundary.
If they keep pushing, walk away.
If they guilt-trip you, let them be uncomfortable.

You are not responsible for how other people feel about your limits.

4. Silence Is Your Superpower

A lot of people struggle with boundaries because they feel the need to over-explain themselves.

So when they say no, they keep talking.

> ▸ *"I can't help out this weekend because I have a lot going on, and I've been really overwhelmed, and I need to catch up on sleep, and also my cousin's in town so I might need to see them, and I just really need a break, but if you really need me, I guess I could..."*

STOP.

The more you talk, the more people will look for a weak spot to argue with.

Say your boundary.
Then shut up.

If they try to guilt-trip you? Let them sit in it.
If they try to negotiate? Let the silence do the talking.
If they get mad? That's a them problem, not a you problem.

What Happens When You Start Enforcing Boundaries

At first, setting boundaries will feel awkward.

You will feel like you're letting people down.
You will feel like you're being "cold."
You will feel the urge to explain yourself into oblivion.

But something else will happen, too.

1. **Your energy will come back.**
   No more overcommitting. No more doing things you hate just to keep the peace.

2. **You will stop resenting people.**
   When you stop agreeing to things you don't want to do, you stop feeling bitter toward the people asking.
3. **You will start attracting people who respect you.**
   And you'll lose the ones who were only there because you had no boundaries. Good. Let them go.
4. **You will finally feel in control of your own damn life.**
   Because for the first time, you are choosing where your energy goes.

The People Who Don't Like Your Boundaries Are the Reason You Need Them

Let's get real for a second.

The first time you set a boundary with someone who was benefiting from your lack of one, they will not like it.

They might get upset.
They might guilt-trip you.
They might say you've changed.

And you have.

You've stopped letting people take advantage of your time.
You've stopped bending over backward to make everyone else comfortable while making yourself miserable.
You've stopped saying yes when you mean no.

And if someone only wants you in their life when you're available to them 24/7, then they don't actually care about *you.*

They care about what you can do for them.

And that? That is not love. That is convenience.

Final Takeaway: Boundaries Are the Highest Form of Self-Respect

You are not responsible for everyone else's comfort.

You are not obligated to be constantly available.

You do not need to sacrifice yourself to be loved, valued, or respected.

Your time is valuable.

Your energy is sacred.

Your peace is non-negotiable.

And anyone who makes you feel guilty for protecting those things?

They are the reason you need boundaries in the first place.

SECTION 3: Boundaries at Work, at Home, and in Your Relationships

There was a time in my life when I thought being available meant being valuable.

I was the person who answered emails at midnight, picked up every call, showed up to every event, and listened to every vent session as if it were my job. Because I thought that's what good people do. Good employees. Good friends. Good daughters. Good partners.

You give. You accommodate. You make yourself useful.

Until one day, I woke up and realized I didn't belong to myself anymore.

I belonged to my inbox.
I belonged to the expectations of people who would take as much as I was willing to give.
I belonged to obligations I never consciously agreed to.

And I wondered why I was exhausted.

The Subtle Theft of Your Time and Energy

Losing yourself doesn't happen in some dramatic, movie-style breakdown. It happens in small, quiet moments of surrender.

It happens when you stay late at work "just this once."
When you agree to plans you don't want to go to because *"they'd be disappointed if you didn't."*
When you say, *"It's fine, I'll handle it,"* for the hundredth time.

And at first, you don't mind.
At first, it feels good to be needed.

Until it doesn't.

Until one day, you catch yourself sighing before answering the phone because you know the conversation is going to drain you.

Until you stop checking your messages because you already know there's going to be a request hidden inside.

Until every part of your life starts to feel like a list of obligations instead of a life you actually want to be living.

That's when you realize: Boundaries aren't selfish. They're the only way to stay whole.

Boundaries at Work – The Hustle That Won't Love You Back

Let's talk about your job.

The place that promises you *"We're like a family here,"* while treating you like a machine.

The place that says *"We appreciate you,"* but hands you more work instead of a raise.

The place that will replace you in two weeks if you drop dead, but will happily let you work yourself into the ground while you're still breathing.

At work, boundaries are the difference between having a career and being consumed by one.

Because if you don't set them?

Work will take over everything.

Your evenings. Your weekends. Your ability to enjoy a meal without checking your phone.

And the worst part? You'll think it's your fault.

You'll tell yourself you need to manage your time better.

That if you were just *a little more efficient,* maybe you wouldn't feel like you're drowning.

That everyone else seems to be handling it, so maybe you're just weak.

No.

You're not weak. You're overextended. And the only way to fix that is to stop allowing it.

How to Take Your Time Back Without Losing Your Job

- ▶ If you don't want to work outside of hours, stop answering emails outside of hours.
- ▶ If they try to give you more work, ask what you should deprioritize. ("I'd be happy to take this on. What should I push back?")
- ▶ If you need a day off, take it—without guilt, without apology, without checking in.

No one is going to tell you when to stop. You have to decide for yourself.

Because let me promise you this: No one will remember how many hours you put in. But you? You will remember every single thing you missed because of work.

Boundaries with Family – Love Doesn't Mean Obligation

I grew up believing that family comes first.

It sounds good in theory. But what happens when *"family comes first"* means you always come last?

What happens when it means picking up the phone even when you don't want to talk?

What happens when it means showing up, even when every part of you wants to stay home?

What happens when it means listening to the same drama, the same complaints, the same emotional weight that was never yours to carry—but you carry it anyway, because *"that's just what family does."*

But here's what I had to learn the hard way:

You can love your family without letting them drain you.

Love doesn't mean always saying yes.
Love doesn't mean always being available.
Love doesn't mean sacrificing yourself just to keep the peace.

Some people—especially family—will take as much of you as you are willing to give.
And when you finally say, *"I can't do this anymore,"* they won't know what to do with it.

Because they were never expecting you to have limits.

But here's the truth:

If your love is only valuable when it's unlimited, then they weren't loving *you.* They were loving your availability.

And that? That is not love. That is dependency.

Boundaries in Relationships – When Love Becomes a Weight Instead of a Home

There is a fine line between love and self-sacrifice.

And a lot of us don't realize we've crossed it until we're already exhausted.

We think we're just being supportive.
We think we're just being patient.
We think we're just doing what good partners do.

And then one day, we realize:

We are no longer in a relationship. We are in a full-time emotional labor job with no benefits, no PTO, and no way out.

If you have ever felt like you are:

> The one always carrying the weight of the relationship.

> The one who gives more, forgives more, understands more.

> The one who has to manage not only your own emotions but theirs too.

Then you already know why boundaries in relationships matter.

Because love should not feel like a never-ending task list.
Because you should not be more tired than happy.
Because you are not a rehabilitation center for someone else's emotional wounds.

And if your relationship only thrives when you abandon your own needs, then it's not a relationship. It's self-abandonment with a romantic filter.

How to Set Boundaries in Relationships Without Losing Yourself

> If you need space, say so. ("I love you, but I need some time to myself tonight.")

> If you feel like you're carrying everything, speak up. ("I can't be the only one putting in the effort here.")

> If your boundaries are ignored, recognize it for what it is—not a misunderstanding, but a choice.

Because at the end of the day, love should be expansive. It should make you feel more like yourself, not less.

And if a relationship only works when you have no boundaries, then it doesn't work at all.

Final Takeaway: Boundaries Are the Fastest Way to Find Out Who Actually Respects You

At first, setting boundaries will feel like breaking something.

Like breaking your habits.
Like breaking your relationships.
Like breaking the version of yourself that was so easy to take advantage of.

But what you're really doing?

You're breaking the cycle that made you think exhaustion was normal.

And when you do?

You'll see who actually loves you for you.

Because the people who truly care? They will respect your boundaries. The ones who don't? They will resent them.

Let them.

Because your peace is worth more than anyone's temporary disappointment.

SECTION 4: What Happens When You Actually Stick to Your Boundaries

There is a moment—after you set a boundary, after you stand your ground, after you choose yourself—when the air feels different. Lighter.

It's unsettling at first, the way silence follows where you used to rush in with "Sure, I can do that."

It's strange, how a request sits unanswered, how a demand is met with stillness instead of your usual over-giving, over-explaining, over-committing.

And then, suddenly, you realize—this is what freedom feels like.

Not the loud, rebellious kind. Not the kind that requires running away or cutting people off. The quiet kind.

The kind where you don't flinch when your phone rings.
The kind where you wake up without dread.
The kind where your time, your energy, your emotions are yours again.

And you wonder why it took you so damn long to get here.

When the Fear Fades, the Power Rushes In

At first, boundaries feel terrifying. Like stepping onto a stage you never rehearsed for, heart pounding, waiting for the world to tell you you're wrong for wanting peace.

But then—you realize something shocking.

The world does not collapse when you say no.

> The friend who always expected you to drop everything? They find someone else.

> The boss who relied on your unpaid overtime? They figure it out.

The family member who guilt-tripped you? They adjust. Or they don't. Either way, you stop bending to it.

You stop over-explaining.
You stop negotiating your own comfort.
You stop feeling like you owe people more of yourself than you want to give.

And what fills the space where exhaustion used to live?

Relief. Clarity. Power.

You start to realize:

You don't have to be constantly available to be valuable.

You don't have to prove your worth by overextending yourself.

You don't have to manage people's disappointment to deserve peace.

And once you get a taste of this kind of freedom, you never go back.

The First Time You Experience Peace, You'll Mourn the Years You Lived Without It

There will come a day—sooner than you think—when you sit alone, and instead of resentment, exhaustion, or guilt, you feel something unfamiliar.

Stillness.

No obligations creeping into your mind.
No tightness in your chest from stretching yourself too thin.
No running mental tally of what you *should* be doing for someone else.

And that's when it will hit you:

This is what it means to belong to yourself.

And for a moment, your stomach will drop—not from fear, but from grief.

Because you will suddenly understand just how long you lived without this.

How many years you spent saying yes when you meant no.
How much energy you wasted making sure everyone else was comfortable while you were slowly drowning.
How deeply you betrayed yourself, not out of malice, but out of a misguided belief that being good meant being available.

That grief will be sharp.
But it will not last.

Because after the grief? Comes something else.

Something stronger.

Determination.

The iron-clad knowing that you will never, ever let yourself live like that again.

What Happens When You Become "The Person with Boundaries"

At first, people will be confused.
Then, some will be angry.
Then, the ones who never planned on respecting you in the first place?

They'll leave.

And this is where a lot of people panic.

"What if I lose people?"
"What if they don't like the new me?"
"What if I end up alone?"

But here's the truth:

You are not losing people. You are losing the illusion that they cared about you as a whole person, instead of just what you could do for them.

And the people who stay?

They will respect you.
They will adjust.
They will recognize that the version of you who set themselves on fire to keep others warm is gone.

And good. That version of you needed to go.

Because the real you? The free you?

That person has better things to do than prove their worth through exhaustion.

Final Takeaway: Boundaries Don't Make Life Smaller—They Make It Yours Again

People think boundaries are about keeping things out.
But the truth?

Boundaries are about making room for the things that matter.

For joy.
For peace.
For a life that feels full instead of drained.

The people who truly love you?
They will not leave just because you have limits.

And the ones who do?
You are better off without them.

Because you were never meant to live at the mercy of other people's expectations.

You were meant to live.

And for the first time, you finally are.

CHAPTER
05

People Are Gonna People

There is one universal truth about life: People are gonna people.

No matter how much you explain yourself, no matter how much you try to be clear, kind, accommodating, or do things the right way, people will still react however they want.

Some will love you. Some will misunderstand you. Some will never be satisfied no matter what you do.

And if you are constantly bending, shrinking, and twisting yourself to control other people's reactions, you are going to spend your entire life exhausted, resentful, and still disappointing people anyway.

Because you cannot control people.

Not their opinions. Not their expectations. Not their assumptions. Not how they interpret your words, your choices, or your boundaries.

And the moment you stop trying?

You become untouchable.

This chapter is about letting go of the need to manage people's perceptions so you can finally live for yourself.

Let's break it into four sections.

SECTION 1: The Illusion of Influence— Why You Never Really Controlled How People See You

At some point in life, most of us develop a quiet, persistent obsession: managing how others perceive us.

Not in a vain, superficial way. Not always for approval or admiration. But for something far deeper—to control the narrative of who we are.

We curate. We soften our edges. We explain ourselves even when no one asked. We anticipate how people might misunderstand us and adjust accordingly.

Why? Because we believe that if we can just get people to see us the right way, then we will be safe. We will be loved. We will be understood.

This is one of the greatest illusions of human existence.

Because no matter how carefully you choose your words,
No matter how much context you provide,
No matter how many times you clarify your intentions,

People will still see what they are ready to see.

Not what is real.
Not what is true.
Not even what you have explicitly told them.

But what fits inside the framework of their experiences, their biases, their fears, their unresolved wounds.

This is not something you can change.
And more importantly, this is not something you were ever meant to control.

The Myth of the "Right" Version of You

Most of us believe—consciously or not—that there is a right way to exist in the eyes of others.

That if we are just kind enough, clear enough, careful enough, then people will get it.

But here's the truth no one tells you:

You can do everything "right" and still be misinterpreted.

You can be the most well-intentioned person in the world and still be misunderstood.

You can lay out your truth as plainly as possible, and people will still project onto you whatever their mind needs to believe.

Because perception is not objective.

It is a reflection of the perceiver, not the perceived.

What they see in you is often a mirror of what they refuse to see in themselves.

So when someone sees your confidence as arrogance,

Your boundaries as coldness,

Your ambition as selfishness,

It's not necessarily because that's who you are.

It's because that's how their mind categorizes what it doesn't understand.

The Framework Problem—Why People Can Only See What Fits Their Worldview

Humans do not like cognitive dissonance.

We like things that make sense according to the frameworks we already hold.

So when something—or someone—doesn't fit our understanding, we do one of two things:

1. **We adjust our framework.** (Rare, uncomfortable, requires real self-awareness.)
2. **We force the person or idea to fit the closest category in our mind—even if it's wrong.** (Much easier, much more common.)

Most people will choose the second option.

Not because they're malicious. Not because they want to misunderstand you. But because understanding requires effort, and effort requires discomfort, and most people are already too overwhelmed to challenge their own thinking.

So they take shortcuts.

They take the easiest, fastest, most accessible explanation and run with it.

And you? You are not responsible for breaking apart their mental shortcuts.

You are not responsible for making yourself digestible to people who refuse to chew.

The Paradox of Acceptance—How Letting Go Gives You Back Your Power

The more energy you spend trying to control how people see you, the more trapped you become.

Because the real prison is not their judgment.
The real prison is the belief that if you just worked harder, explained better, edited more, then maybe—maybe—you could make them understand.

This is a trap.

Because the more effort you put into managing perceptions, the more you reinforce the idea that their perception is your responsibility.

It is not.

What they see is the sum total of their own life experiences, not yours.

And when you finally accept that?
When you finally stop chasing clarity in other people's minds?
When you finally allow yourself to be misunderstood, misinterpreted, mislabeled, and still remain whole?

You reclaim your energy.

You stop spending your time rewriting your existence to fit someone else's expectations.

You stop performing for an audience that was never actually watching.

You stop filtering your truth in the hopes that someone else will see it clearly.

And in that moment, you become free.

Final Takeaway: The End of Image Management

You never had control over how people saw you.
You never had control over how they interpreted your actions.
You never had control over how they processed your words, your choices, your boundaries.

All you ever had control over?

Was your own clarity.

So instead of wasting energy on being "understood,"
Instead of bending, shifting, and filtering yourself to avoid judgment,
Instead of hoping that if you just explain it well enough, people will finally get it—

Let it go.

Because at the end of your life, the only person who will have lived with your choices,
The only person who will have carried the weight of your compromises,
The only person who will have known what it cost you to shape yourself into what others needed—

Is you.

And you deserve to live a life that feels like your own.

SECTION 2: The People Who Judge You Aren't Doing Any Better

There is an invisible contract we all sign at some point in life.

It says: If you do things the way they've always been done, you will be accepted. If you step outside of that, you will be questioned.

Nobody hands you this contract outright. You don't sign it with a pen. But you agree to it every time you shrink yourself to avoid discomfort, every time you hold your tongue when you should have spoken, every time you adjust your decisions to avoid being "too much" for someone else.

Then, one day, you wake up and realize you don't remember ever deciding who you wanted to be—you only remember reacting to who people expected you to be.

And the second you start choosing differently?
The second you start reclaiming your time, your space, your life?

People will notice.

And not all of them will approve.

This is where most people stop.
Not because they want to, but because the weight of judgment is too much to bear.

But before you let their opinions pull you back into a life that does not belong to you, you have to ask yourself a question:

Who are you letting define you?

And more importantly—why do you trust them to?

The Unqualified Judges of Your Life

Imagine sitting in a courtroom where the judge knows nothing about law.

They've never studied a case. They don't understand evidence. They have no credentials.
And yet—they are in charge of your verdict.

Would you accept their ruling?
Would you let them decide your fate?
Would you adjust your choices based on their misunderstanding of reality?

No. That would be absurd.

So why do we let unqualified people pass judgment on our lives?

Why do we let:

> People who have never built anything tell us how to run our careers?

> People who have never known peace tell us how to handle conflict?

> People who are afraid to take risks tell us what's "realistic"?

We act as if judgment is evidence when, most of the time, it's just projection.

And yet, we let it shape us.

We let people who have never lived a day in our experience define who we are.

What would happen if we stopped?

What would happen if, instead of taking their opinions as truth, we saw them for what they really are—a reflection of their own limitations, not ours?

Why People Critique What They Cannot Do Themselves

When you start changing—whether that means setting boundaries, taking risks, or stepping into yourself in a way you never have before—there will always be people who try to pull you back.

Not because they hate you. Not even because they want to hurt you. But because your growth highlights their stagnation.

People who have spent their entire lives avoiding their own potential will resent those who embrace theirs.

Not openly, not directly. But subtly.
Through side comments, dismissiveness, passive-aggressive concern.

"You're really gonna do that?"

"That seems a little unrealistic."

"You've changed."

Pay attention to these moments.

Because what they are really saying is:

"I don't understand this because I have never allowed myself to try."

"If this works for you, I have to question why I never pursued it myself."

"I liked you better when you played by the rules I understood."

It is not about you.
It is about the discomfort your existence creates for them.

And the second you recognize that, their judgment loses its power.

The Emotional Intelligence to See Beyond the Judgment

The easiest response to judgment is defensiveness.
The most evolved response is understanding.

Not for them—for you.

Because when you start to see judgment for what it really is, you stop reacting to it as if it's a personal attack.

You stop explaining yourself to people who are not willing to listen.
You stop feeling the need to prove your worth to people who have already decided who you are.
You stop internalizing rejection as a reflection of your inadequacy.

Because rejection does not mean you are wrong.
It does not mean you have failed.
It does not mean you should reconsider.

Rejection is often just proof that you are doing something different.

And in a world where so many people live in quiet discontent, doing something different will always make people uncomfortable.

So let them misunderstand.
Let them doubt.
Let them judge.

And then—do it anyway.

Because the person who is truly free is not the one who is liked by everyone.

It's the one who no longer needs to be.

SECTION 3: **The Mind's Need for Certainty— Why People Will Misunderstand You Anyway**

There is something terrifying about being misrepresented.

Something primal, something buried deep in the oldest part of the human brain—the part that still thinks we live in caves, that exile means death, that being misunderstood is a threat to our survival.

Because, at one point in history, it was.

When we lived in tightly bonded tribes, being seen accurately wasn't a luxury; it was a necessity. If people misunderstood your intentions, they could banish you. If they questioned your loyalty, they could turn against you.

And so, the brain evolved to obsess over clarity, over being properly interpreted, over controlling how others perceive us.

Fast forward to today, and that instinct is still alive. The world has changed, but your brain hasn't gotten the memo.

So when someone misjudges you, dismisses you, or distorts your words, that ancient fear flares up like an alarm you can't shut off.

And what do we do? We panic. We explain. We fight for understanding like our lives depend on it.

Even when it's pointless.
Even when the person we're talking to has already made up their mind.
Even when the battle isn't worth the energy we're spending.

Because at the end of the day, we are wired to crave certainty.

And being misunderstood? That is uncertainty in its most personal form.

The Brain's Compulsion to Fill in the Gaps

Here's something most people don't realize:

When the brain encounters an incomplete story, it doesn't just sit with the unknown.

It fills in the gaps.

It takes whatever fragmented information it has, pulls from past experiences, biases, and beliefs, and builds a version of reality that it can live with.

This is called cognitive closure.

It's why your mind turns a shadow in the hallway into a human figure when you're home alone.
It's why you assume the person who didn't text back is ignoring you, even if their phone is dead.
It's why people make snap judgments about you based on the tiniest slivers of information.

Because uncertainty is uncomfortable. So the brain avoids it at all costs.

And when someone doesn't have enough context about you?

They do not ask questions.
They do not wait for clarification.
They fill in the blanks with whatever makes the most sense to them.

Even if it's wrong.

Even if it reduces you to a version that has nothing to do with who you actually are.

Even if it is so far from the truth that you want to scream.

And the worst part?

Once the brain creates a narrative, it defends it.

That's why people cling to their first impressions, even when they're wrong.
That's why explaining yourself often doesn't change anything.
That's why the more you try to prove someone wrong about you, the harder they resist.

Their brain is protecting its version of reality.

And that version of reality?

It has nothing to do with you.

You Are a Collection of Stories—But You Don't Get to Write Them All

Think about how many different versions of you exist in the world.

To one person, you are brilliant.
To another, you are arrogant.
To one, you are kind.
To another, you are too soft.
To one, you are unforgettable.
To another, you are barely a passing thought.

And the truth?

None of them are wrong.
And none of them are completely right.

Because you are not one thing. You are not one sentence, one moment, one decision, one mistake.

You are an entire, ever-changing, multidimensional human being.

But people? They don't have time for multidimensional.
They don't have time to sit with complexity, to let you be a full person.

So they reduce you.

They take the version of you that is most convenient for their story,
Most comfortable for their worldview,
Most useful for the role they need you to play.

And then?

They never think to question it.

Because questioning it would mean holding space for a reality that is more complex than they are willing to deal with.

The Moment You Realize You Don't Owe Anyone an Explanation

There comes a moment—sometimes after years of battling other people's perceptions—when it finally clicks:

You never had control over their opinions in the first place.

Not really.
Not in any meaningful way.

Sure, you could correct them.
You could over-explain yourself into exhaustion.
You could write them a detailed manual on who you are, laminated and perfectly formatted.

But they will still see what they want to see.

Because their version of you is not built on facts.
It is built on what their brain needs to believe.

And the moment you stop trying to control that?

You get something most people will never have.

Freedom.

Freedom from justifying yourself.
Freedom from rewriting yourself to fit their comfort.
Freedom from playing defense in a game where the rules are stacked against you.

Because you cannot win a battle against someone else's mental shortcuts. And the good news?

You don't have to.

Because the people who actually matter? They will always ask for the full story.

And the ones who don't? They were never truly looking at you anyway.

Final Takeaway: Not Everyone Deserves the Full Story of You

Most people do not see you.

They see what their brain has decided you are.
They see a summary, a shortcut, a simplification.
And they will judge you based on that.

But here is what you need to know:

You are not required to spend your life correcting them.

You are allowed to walk away from a version of yourself that someone else created.
You are allowed to exist without making yourself digestible.
You are allowed to be misjudged and still be whole.

Because if someone is committed to misunderstanding you?
You will exhaust yourself trying to prove them wrong.

And the cost of that exhaustion?
Is your own clarity.

And between their false perception and your peace?
You should always choose your peace.

SECTION 4: **The Space You Gain—How Letting Go Reshapes Your Life**

There is something no one tells you about letting go: it does not leave you empty. It fills you.

When you finally stop gripping other people's opinions like they are the air you breathe, when you step out of the exhausting role of self-appointed reputation manager, when you no longer shape yourself based on how others might receive you—you don't lose yourself. You find yourself.

But more than that, you find space.

Space to actually manage your life, to focus on what matters, to fully show up for what is in front of you instead of being mentally shackled to what someone might be thinking about you in the background.

This is not some abstract, feel-good notion. It is tangible, measurable, real.

Letting go of what you cannot control does not leave you wandering. It organizes you.

It puts your energy back where it belongs.

And when that happens? Your entire life becomes easier to manage.

Your Energy Comes Back—And You Finally Have Enough for What Matters

Most people don't realize how much of their energy is being stolen by conversations they aren't even having.

Replaying what you should have said.
Anticipating what someone might think.
Preparing defenses for arguments that may never happen.

It is a constant, background process running in your mind, draining your battery.

And when you finally release that?

> You wake up with clarity instead of tension.

> You walk into rooms without needing to analyze how people perceive you.

> You move through your day without carrying invisible debates in your head.

And suddenly, you have energy again.

Not just to get through the day, but to fully engage with it.

To pour into the things that actually deserve your attention.
To manage your life, instead of spending all your energy managing other people's perceptions of you.

And this is the moment you realize:

The exhaustion you thought was from work, or from stress, or from just being an adult—so much of it was coming from the weight of carrying things that were never yours to carry.

Your Decision-Making Becomes Effortless

When you stop factoring in imaginary opinions, decision-making becomes infinitely easier.

Because let's be honest—half the reason most people feel stuck in life isn't because they don't know what to do.

It's because they are making decisions for an audience.

> *What will they think if I quit?*

What if they judge me for saying no?

What if people think I'm selfish for choosing this path?

And so, every decision gets weighed down. Not just by the practical factors but by the mental gymnastics of predicting how it will be received.

But when you let that go?

> You make choices faster because you aren't stopping to calculate how they will be perceived.

> You become decisive because you are finally making choices based on what serves you, not what keeps everyone else comfortable.

> You move without hesitation because you no longer have to filter your instincts through the imagined reactions of people who aren't living your life.

It is liberating.
It is efficient.
It is how you were always meant to live.

You Become a Better Problem Solver

Most people think letting go means disengaging from life.
That it makes you passive, detached, less involved.

But the opposite is true.

Letting go doesn't make you weaker—it makes you sharper.

Because when you are not spending half your mental energy worrying about things outside of your control, you have more capacity to handle what actually needs your attention.

Suddenly, you:

- ▶ Solve problems at work without second-guessing yourself.
- ▶ Manage conflicts without the emotional drain of worrying about whether you'll be judged for handling them "wrong."
- ▶ Handle stress with actual resilience, because you are no longer exhausting yourself on irrelevant concerns.

This is how leaders operate.

Not by being indifferent.
Not by ignoring everything.
But by channeling their energy only into what actually moves the needle.

And this is why people who let go of unnecessary worries tend to rise faster in their careers, in their businesses, in their personal lives.

Because they are no longer operating on mental clutter.

Your Personal Relationships Become Healthier—And Less Exhausting

When you are no longer consumed by how you are being perceived, your relationships change in ways you never expected.

Suddenly, you:

Listen better because you are not formulating the perfect response in your head.

Communicate more clearly because you are not editing yourself into something palatable.

Attract people who actually align with you—not just the version of you that performed for approval.

And here's the most unexpected part:

When you stop shaping yourself to fit other people's expectations, you start to notice who actually values you for who you are.

> Some relationships will fade, because they were built on your compliance.

> Some friendships will shift, because they depended on your willingness to overextend.

> Some people will be uncomfortable, because they benefited from your exhaustion.

But the relationships that remain?
The ones that strengthen?

Those are real.

Because they are built on who you actually are—not who you performed yourself into being.

And for the first time, you will understand what it feels like to be loved without condition.

You Stop Feeling Like Life Is Slipping Away from You

You don't realize how much time and opportunity you've lost until you stop letting external worries run your life.

You don't realize how many dreams you postponed
How many moments you missed
How many things you could have built, created, and experienced

If only you had put your energy where it actually mattered.

And when you finally stop managing perceptions?

When you take all of that energy back?

You start to understand just how much was stolen from you.

By worry.
By hesitation.
By the lie that you had to shape yourself into something digestible before you were worthy of showing up fully.

This is when life speeds up in the best way.

Because you are no longer delaying, waiting, tiptoeing around your own existence.

You are finally, fully in it.

And for the first time, you are actually living.

Final Takeaway: The Life You Want is on the Other Side of Letting Go

Letting go is not about indifference.

It is not about apathy.

It is not about ignoring everything and living in some passive state of nonchalance.

It is about strategy.

It is about recognizing that your energy, your time, your decisions, and your mental space are limited resources.

And wasting them on things that are out of your control?

That is the fastest way to live a small, exhausted, unfulfilled life.

But when you stop?

When you reclaim all of that energy?

> Everything changes.
> You move faster.
> You think clearer.
> You solve problems instead of marinating in them.
> You make decisions without fear.
> You live instead of hesitating.

Because the life you want? The one that feels full, aligned, expansive, effortless?

It is waiting for you.

On the other side of letting go.

CHAPTER

06

The Productivity Scam

We were sold a lie.

Somewhere along the way, we were told that the key to a meaningful life is optimization. That the secret to success is to squeeze every ounce of usefulness out of our time. That if we just wake up earlier, work harder, eliminate distractions, and keep grinding, we will finally reach some mythical place where we can rest.

But what happens when we actually get there?

The finish line moves.
The workload increases.
The reward for productivity is more work.

And before we even realize what's happened, we become workers first, humans second.

This is the productivity scam: the illusion that if you just do enough, achieve enough, hustle enough, you will finally feel worthy.

This chapter is about unraveling that illusion—and what happens when you finally step off the hamster wheel.

SECTION 1: The Illusion of Productivity— Why You're Always Busy but Never Fulfilled

Most people don't realize they're trapped in a productivity loop until it's too late.

At first, it feels good. Checking boxes. Completing tasks. Crossing things off lists. Productivity gives you a dopamine hit, a small rush of achievement that tells you, *Yes, you're on the right track.*

But over time, that feeling fades.

Because productivity—the way we've been taught to define it—is not about creating a meaningful life.

It's about speed.
It's about efficiency.
It's about output.

And in a world where we are expected to maximize every hour, we start believing that the more we do, the more valuable we are.

So we squeeze every ounce of "usefulness" out of our day.

>We listen to self-improvement podcasts while commuting.

>We turn hobbies into side hustles.

>We track, measure, and optimize even our leisure time.

Because we have been conditioned to believe that existing isn't enough—we must justify our existence through productivity.

But here's the thing:

You are not tired because you're doing too little.
You are tired because you are doing too much of what doesn't matter.

And if you don't change how you define productivity, you will spend your entire life running in circles, working harder but never feeling any closer to fulfillment.

The Real Problem: You're Optimizing the Wrong Things

Most people assume that if they are exhausted, they just need to manage their time better.

So they buy planners, download scheduling apps, read books on efficiency.

They try to pack their schedules tighter, cut out wasted minutes, and push themselves to "do more in less time."

But here's the problem:

You do not have a time management issue.
You have an energy misallocation issue.

Because productivity is not just about what you do.
It's about what those tasks actually contribute to your life.

Think about it:

> If you spend hours responding to emails but make no real progress on meaningful work, were you actually productive?

> If you spend all day in meetings that could have been resolved with a two-sentence email, did you use your time wisely?

> If you check off every task on your list but feel no closer to the life you want, was it worth the effort?

Because not all tasks are equal.

And productivity without intention is just busywork.

The Productivity Audit—How to Identify Where Your Time is Being Wasted

If you want to actually reclaim your time and energy, you need to audit how you're spending them.

Not theoretically. Not vaguely. With brutal honesty.

For one week, track every hour of your day.
Not what you *think* you do—but what you *actually* do.

Then, break everything down into three categories:

1. **High-Impact Work (Moves You Forward)**
    ▶ These are the things that create real progress.
    ▶ They build, improve, or change something in your life.
    ▶ They contribute to long-term goals, deep fulfillment, and personal growth.

Examples:

    ▶ Learning a high-value skill.
    ▶ Deep focus on a meaningful project.
    ▶ Investing in relationships that nourish you.

2. **Maintenance Work (Keeps You Running but Doesn't Move You Forward)**
    ▶ These are necessary but should not consume the majority of your time.
    ▶ They keep life functioning, but they don't create significant change.

Examples:

    ▶ Checking emails.
    ▶ Grocery shopping, laundry, cleaning.
    ▶ Administrative tasks that don't require deep thought.

3. **Low-Value Work (Looks Productive But Isn't)**
    ▶ These are the things that feel like work but don't actually contribute to your goals.
    ▶ They drain energy without giving real results.

Examples:

    ▶ Repetitive tasks that could be automated.
    ▶ Meetings that serve no real purpose.
    ▶ Over-explaining, overthinking, and doing unnecessary work out of habit.

Once you have your breakdown, calculate how much time you are spending in each category.

Chances are, you are spending 80% of your time on low-impact work.
Which means you are not busy with progress.
You are busy with distractions.

And that? That is the reason why you are exhausted.

The Productivity Shift—How to Focus Only on What Actually Matters

If you want to escape the productivity scam, you need to make one fundamental shift:

Stop measuring success by how much you get done.
Start measuring it by how much of it actually matters.

This means:

> Cutting out tasks that do not serve a real purpose.

> Batching low-energy work instead of letting it eat up your best hours.

> Saying no to "urgent" but unimportant tasks that keep you in reaction mode.

> Structuring your day around deep, high-value work instead of trying to fit it in between distractions.

This is not about doing less.
This is about doing the right things with more focus, more energy, and more presence.

Because a well-managed life is not one that is perfectly scheduled.
It is one where your time is spent where it actually belongs.

The Difference Between Being Busy and Being Effective

Let's be clear:

The world will reward you for being busy.

Your boss will be impressed by how quickly you respond to emails.
Your colleagues will admire how packed your schedule is.
Society will pat you on the back for being overworked.

But your body? Your mind? Your soul?

They will beg you to stop.

Because deep down, you know the truth:

Being busy is not the same as being effective.

Busy people:

> Do everything but accomplish little.
> Feel exhausted but unfulfilled.
> Look successful but feel trapped.

Effective people:

> Do fewer things but execute them well.
> Manage their time around energy, not tasks.
> Prioritize meaningful work over the illusion of progress.

And at the end of the day?

The ones who are truly successful are not the ones who worked the hardest.

They are the ones who worked on the right things, in the right way, at the right time.

Because real productivity isn't about doing more.

It's about making space for what actually matters.

SECTION 2: **Energy Is Currency— Spend It Wisely**

We treat time like currency, but it's energy that actually pays for everything.

Time is passive. You can sit in a room for eight hours and get nothing done. You can spend all day "working" and move no closer to what actually matters. But energy is active. It is what powers execution, what moves ideas from thoughts into reality, what determines whether an hour is wasted or maximized.

Yet, we spend energy like it's unlimited, like we can just keep pulling from the same well no matter how much we've depleted it. We believe that as long as there are hours left in the day, we should be able to push through.

But this is a lie.

Because energy is not time. It is currency.

And like any currency, if you spend it carelessly, you will run out.

Understanding Your Energy Bank—Why Not All Hours Are Equal

Imagine waking up with a set amount of money to spend each day.

Some people wake up with $100 of energy. They slept well, they're healthy, their mental load is low.
Some people wake up with $30. They're stressed, sleep-deprived, mentally stretched thin.
Some people wake up with $10. Running on fumes, held together by caffeine and obligation.

And yet, the world expects all of us to spend the same amount, at the same rate, on the same tasks.

But here's the truth:

▸ A $50 task at the start of the day might only cost you $20. You're fresh, focused, efficient.

▸ That same task at 4 PM, when your energy is drained? It costs you $80. It takes longer, feels harder, and depletes you completely.

▸ Some things don't just take energy. They leak it. An unnecessary meeting, a conversation that drains you, an unresolved conflict sitting in the back of your mind—that's like getting hit with invisible transaction fees all day long.

Most people never track where their energy is going. They only notice when the account is empty—when they're exhausted, unfocused, irritable. And by then? They've already overspent.

How Energy Debt Is Keeping You Stuck

If you consistently spend more energy than you replenish, you go into debt.

And just like financial debt, energy debt compounds.

At first, it just feels like fatigue.
Then, it becomes harder to focus.
Then, you start procrastinating, not because you're lazy, but because you literally don't have the reserves to engage.
Then, motivation disappears.
Then, decision-making starts to feel impossible.

And before you know it, you're stuck in a cycle of exhaustion that no amount of caffeine or time-blocking can fix.

Because time doesn't clear debt.
Rest does.

And rest is not just "not working."
Rest is a deliberate investment into replenishing the energy you've spent.

The Real Productivity Strategy—Spending Energy Like an Investor, Not a Consumer

Most people spend energy like reckless consumers.

They react to demands, say yes to everything, allow themselves to be pulled in every direction.

They throw energy at anything that feels urgent, regardless of whether it actually moves them forward.

They assume that if they just keep pushing, the exhaustion will somehow correct itself.

But the people who are truly productive?

They treat energy like an investment portfolio.

> They allocate their energy toward what gives the highest return.

> They stop spending their best hours on things that deplete them without payoff.

> They diversify how they recharge, so they never hit empty.

Instead of just asking, "What do I have to do today?"

They ask:

"What deserves my best energy?"
"What low-value tasks can be done when I'm running low?"
"How do I ensure my energy doesn't get wasted on things that give me nothing back?"

And that? That is the shift that changes everything.

Because now, you are not just working harder—you are working in a way that is actually sustainable.

How to Manage Your Energy Portfolio Like a High-Performer

There is a simple way to start spending energy intentionally instead of bleeding it out all day.

You divide your tasks into three categories:

1. High-Energy Investments – Tasks that require deep focus, strategic thinking, or creative effort. These need your sharpest energy.
2. Maintenance Transactions – Routine work, admin tasks, emails. These should be batched and handled during your lower-energy periods.
3. Energy Leaks – Unnecessary obligations, constant social media checking, unresolved stressors. These should be eliminated or automated.

Then, you align your energy spending with your actual reserves.

▶ Do your highest-energy tasks when your cognitive account is full.
▶ Push low-return work to times when you are naturally depleted.
▶ Stop making major withdrawals on an empty account.

This is not just about avoiding burnout.

This is about making sure that the energy you spend actually gets you somewhere.

Because working harder in low-energy states is not productivity.

It is operating at a loss.

What Happens When You Stop Overspending Your Energy

The moment you stop wasting your best energy on the wrong things, everything changes.

You get more done in fewer hours.
You stop feeling like you're constantly behind.
You stop dreading work because it no longer feels like you're pushing through a fog of exhaustion.

And more than anything?

You start living with capacity.

Capacity to think clearly.
Capacity to enjoy your free time without guilt.
Capacity to actually be present in your own life.

Because that's what energy management really gives you.

Not just more efficiency.
Not just better performance.
But the ability to move through life without constantly running on empty.

And that? That is real productivity.

Because a person who knows how to spend their energy wisely will always outperform the person who is just trying to fit more into their day.

Final Takeaway: Treat Your Energy Like a Limited Budget—Because It Is

Stop working harder.

Stop scheduling tasks without thinking about what they actually cost.

Stop assuming that just because there are hours left in the day, you should keep pushing.

Start asking:

"Is this worth the energy it costs me?"

"Am I spending my best energy on the things that truly matter?"

"What would happen if I stopped draining myself on things that give me nothing in return?"

Because if you are not managing your energy, you are not actually managing your life.

SECTION 3: **The 7-Day Anti-Productivity Reset**

A challenge to break free from the productivity trap, reclaim your time, and reset your energy

How This Works:

For the next seven days, you are going to unlearn everything you thought you knew about productivity.

You are going to strip away the unnecessary, eliminate distractions, and reset your mind to work in a way that actually serves you.

Each day comes with an interactive task—not just something to read, but something to do.

No skipping. No rushing. No "I'll do this later."

This is your life, your time, your energy.

Let's take it back.

Day 1: The Energy Audit

What are you actually spending your time on?

Task:

For one full day, track everything you do. Every email. Every text. Every meeting. Every errand. Every moment spent scrolling. Every minute lost to distractions. Write it all down.

At the end of the day, break it down into three categories:

1. Moves me forward – These tasks help build the life I actually want.
2. Keeps me running – These tasks maintain daily life but don't create real change.
3. Wastes my time & energy – These tasks feel productive but give nothing back.

Reflection:

- What percentage of my time is spent on things that actually move me forward?
- What do I need to cut, delegate, or automate to stop wasting energy on low-impact tasks?

Write down one thing you will immediately stop doing.

Day 2: The Productivity Detox

Eliminate fake work. Cut what isn't necessary.

TASK:

Look at yesterday's list. Highlight everything that could be eliminated without consequence.

Now, stop doing those things.

- Cancel a meeting that doesn't need to happen.
- Ignore an email that doesn't need a response.
- Delete a task from your to-do list that is just busywork.

REFLECTION:

- What was I doing just because I thought I *should*?
- How much of my day was filled with things that didn't actually matter?

Write down one task you will never waste time on again.

Day 3: The Anti-Hustle Experiment

Do half as much and see what happens.

TASK:

Pick an area of your life—work, social obligations, errands—and do 50% less than you normally would.

- ▶ Respond to fewer emails.
- ▶ Say no to a commitment.
- ▶ End your workday earlier than usual.
- ▶ Then, observe.

REFLECTION:

- ▶ Did anything actually fall apart?
- ▶ What changed? What didn't?
- ▶ What did I assume was urgent, but really wasn't?

Write down one area of your life where you will permanently do less.

Day 4: The Boundary Test

Say NO without an explanation.

TASK:

Find one thing—an invitation, a request, an expectation—that you do not want to do.

Say no.

- ▶ No apology.
- ▶ No excuse.
- ▶ No justifying.

Just: "I can't."

Then, sit with the discomfort. Notice what it feels like to say no without guilt.

REFLECTION:

- ▶ What did saying no reveal about my fears?
- ▶ How much of my time is controlled by the expectations of others?

Write down one thing you will no longer agree to just because you feel obligated.

Day 5: The Slow Work Challenge

One thing at a time. No distractions.

TASK:

Pick one task today.

- ▶ Work, reading, writing—anything that requires focus.
- ▶ Do it with your full attention.
- ▶ No switching tabs. No checking your phone. No multitasking.

REFLECTION:

- ▶ How did it feel to focus on just one thing?
- ▶ What distractions did I instinctively reach for?

Write down one way you will reduce distractions in your daily life.

Day 6: The White Space Experiment

Do absolutely nothing.

TASK:

For 30 minutes, sit in silence. No phone. No work. No scrolling. No entertainment.

Let the discomfort rise. Feel what it's like to exist without constant input.

REFLECTION:

- ▶ What thoughts surfaced when I had no distractions?
- ▶ What do I avoid when I constantly stay busy?

Write down one way you will create more "white space" in your life.

Day 7: The Reset—Rebuilding A Life That Works For You

Now that you've stripped away the excess, it's time to rebuild.

TASK:

Write down three things you will stop doing forever.
Write down three things you will prioritize moving forward.
Create a schedule that aligns with your energy, not just obligations.

REFLECTION:

- ▶ What have I learned about how I spend my time?
- ▶ What will I do differently from now on?

Write down one sentence that defines how you will live from this moment forward.

The Final Takeaway: You Do Not Need to Earn Your Right to Rest

You do not have to push yourself to exhaustion before you deserve a break.

You do not need to be endlessly productive to prove your worth.

You do not need to measure your life in tasks completed to make it meaningful.

You were never supposed to work like a machine.

You were supposed to live.

And from now on, you will.

JOURNEY JOTS

*Quick, thoughtful notes that document milestones,
insights, and personal growth*

JOURNEY JOTS

Quick, thoughtful notes that document milestones,
insights, and personal growth

_____

_____

_____

_____

_____

_____

_____

_____

_____

_____

_____

_____

_____

_____

_____

JOURNEY JOTS

Quick, thoughtful notes that document milestones, insights, and personal growth

_____

_____

_____

_____

_____

_____

_____

_____

_____

_____

_____

_____

_____

_____

_____

CHAPTER

07

Money, Hustle, and the Art of Not Losing Your Soul

Money is the greatest paradox of modern life.

We need it to survive, yet we are told we should not care too much about it. We chase it to build freedom, yet many people become enslaved to the pursuit of it.

We are encouraged to dream big, hustle hard, and "make it"—but at what cost?

There is a fine line between ambition and self-destruction, between building wealth and being consumed by the process of acquiring it.

Cross that line, and suddenly, you are not working for money—money is working you.

This chapter is about how to make money without letting it make you.

SECTION 1: The Fine Line Between Ambition and Self-Destruction

At first, the hunger feels pure.

You start with nothing but a vision, a drive, a belief that you can build something greater than what you were handed. You push because you have to, because survival demands it, because the alternative—staying small, staying dependent, staying stuck—feels unbearable.

So you hustle.

You wake up earlier, stay up later, work longer. You watch people around you settle into comfort, into predictability, and you tell yourself, *Not me. I will do more. I will be more.*

And for a while, it works.

The late nights pay off. The sacrifices make sense. You taste the first real wins, and the validation rushes in. People start calling you "driven." They admire your work ethic. They ask you how you do it, as if you've cracked some secret formula.

But here's the thing about hunger:

If you don't learn to control it, it will consume you.

The Trap of Never-Enough

Nobody tells you that ambition is a moving target.

That the goalpost does not stay where you left it.

At first, you tell yourself, *If I can just make six figures, I'll be comfortable.* Then you get there, and it's not enough.

You think, *Maybe I just need more.* More income. More deals. More security.

But security is a lie in a world that keeps redefining what success looks like.

You climb higher, but the stakes rise with you.
Your achievements grow, but so do your expenses.
Your status increases, but so does the pressure to maintain it.

And soon, the thing that once made you feel powerful becomes the thing that controls you.

Because the world will never tell you when you have arrived.

There will always be someone ahead of you.
There will always be more you could be doing.
There will always be another level to chase.

And if you are not careful, you will spend your life running toward a finish line that does not exist.

The Body Count of Hustle Culture

Here's what nobody talks about:

For every story of success, there is a story of someone who broke themselves trying to achieve it.

> The entrepreneur who built an empire but lost their family.

> The executive who climbed to the top and still wakes up anxious every morning.

> The workaholic who spent decades grinding, only to realize they don't know who they are outside of their job.

But we don't glorify those stories.

Because society worships outcome over process.

We love the billionaires, the moguls, the icons—but we do not ask what they sacrificed to get there.

We do not ask how many relationships they had to neglect.
We do not ask what their health looked like behind the curtain.
We do not ask if they are even happy with what they built.

Because the truth is, some people don't make it out of ambition alive.

Some wake up too late.

Some don't wake up at all.

And if you don't set your own definition of success—if you do not decide where the line is between ambition and self-destruction—

The world will gladly cross it for you.

The Cost of Living for the Future

For years, I convinced myself that I was working hard so I could finally rest.

I told myself, *Once I hit this goal, then I'll slow down.*
Once I reach this milestone, then I'll enjoy life.
Once I have enough, then I will finally feel secure.

But "enough" is a mirage.

Because the habit of pushing forward does not turn off once you achieve something.

If you do not learn to be present in the life you have now, you will not know how to be present in the life you are working toward.

This is how people spend decades hustling toward a future they never actually get to enjoy.

> They grind through their 20s, saying they'll relax in their 30s.

> They grind through their 30s, saying they'll finally slow down in their 40s.

> They wake up at 50 and realize they spent their best years chasing a peace that never arrived.

Because the mindset that tells you to keep going does not automatically shift into contentment just because you hit a number.

And the scariest part?

If you do not consciously decide where your finish line is, you may never cross it.

The Art of Ambition Without Self-Betrayal

Ambition itself is not the enemy.

Building wealth, achieving goals, creating something bigger than yourself—these are all worthy pursuits.

But if you do not set limits, ambition will take everything you are willing to give.

It will gladly accept your exhaustion.
It will gladly accept your relationships.
It will gladly accept your health, your time, your peace—

Because it does not care what it costs you.

That is your job.

And if you do not define what success looks like before you reach it, you will find yourself achieving things that do not even feel like yours.

This is why ambition must be paired with self-awareness.

> Know what you are working for.

> Know when to push and when to pause.

> Know the difference between working hard to build freedom and working hard just to stay trapped in the game.

Because success is not just about how high you climb.

It is about whether or not you still recognize yourself when you get there.

SECTION 2: Making Money Without Letting It Make You

The first time you make real money, something shifts inside you.

It feels like proof. Proof that you were right to believe in yourself. Proof that the late nights, the sacrifices, the hustle—it wasn't in vain. You start to see the world differently, not in terms of limitations, but in terms of possibilities.

And then, if you're not careful, the fear creeps in.

Because once you start making money, you realize how fragile it feels. You realize that the moment you slow down, you might lose it. You realize that what once felt like freedom now feels like something you have to protect at all costs.

And this is where most people make the fatal mistake.

They do not stop to define the role money plays in their life. They do not stop to ask, *How much is enough?* They do not stop to consider whether they are working for money or if money is now working them.

So instead of using wealth as a tool, they become enslaved to it.

The Psychology of Never-Enough

Most people assume that once they hit a certain income level, they will finally feel secure.

But security is an emotional state, not a financial one.

And money—no matter how much of it you accumulate—does not fix a scarcity mindset.

You see it in people who grind their way into wealth and still act like they're one paycheck away from ruin.

You see it in people who never take breaks because they are afraid to step off the treadmill, even when they have more than enough.

You see it in millionaires who obsessively check their bank accounts, terrified that it will all disappear overnight.

Because here's the truth no one tells you:

If you were anxious about money when you were broke, you will still be anxious about money when you are rich.

Unless you deal with the root of it.

When Money Becomes an Identity Instead of a Tool

Making money changes how people see you.

And if you are not careful, it changes how you see yourself.

Because the moment you become "successful," people treat you differently.

They ask for advice, assuming you have all the answers.
They respect you more, even if you are the same person you were before.
They associate your worth with what you have built, not who you are.

And if you are not conscious of it, you will internalize that identity.

You will start to believe that who you are is tied to what you earn.
You will start to think that if you ever lose your status, your net worth, your momentum—then you lose yourself too.

This is how people become prisoners of their own success.

Not because they need more money.
But because they don't know who they are without it.

How to Make Money Without Losing Yourself

The only way to prevent wealth from becoming a cage is to define its role in your life before you accumulate too much of it to walk away.

Here's how:

1. Set a Clear Definition of "Enough"

Most people never set a financial finish line.

They just assume that more is always better.

But if you never define what "enough" looks like, you will never stop chasing.

> What income level allows you to live comfortably, without overworking?

> What financial goal actually serves your values, instead of just inflating your lifestyle?

> At what point does earning more stop improving your life and just add stress?

If you do not answer these questions, you will be making money out of habit—not out of purpose.

2. Build Wealth to Expand Your Freedom, Not Your Workload

Money is only valuable if it buys you something you actually want.

And what most people want, deep down, is time.

Yet, instead of using money to create space, they use it to trap themselves in more responsibility.

They scale too fast.
They expand too aggressively.

They take on more than they need—not because they want to, but because they are addicted to growth.

And in the process?

They build a business, a career, a life that requires them to keep working at full capacity just to sustain it.

Instead of designing wealth that allows them to step back, they create a system where they can never stop.

That is not success.

That is a sophisticated form of self-inflicted exhaustion.

3. Separate Your Identity From Your Income

You are not your net worth.
You are not your job title.
You are not the number in your bank account.

The moment you let money define who you are, you will make every decision out of fear instead of clarity.

And fear-based decisions?

They are always bad investments.

This is why some of the richest people in the world are the most anxious.

They are no longer just managing money.
They are managing their entire sense of self.

But you are allowed to be a full human being, outside of what you earn.

> You are allowed to make money without it controlling you.

> You are allowed to slow down without losing momentum.

> You are allowed to have ambition without sacrificing your peace.

Because real success is not about accumulating wealth.

It is about building a life that feels rich, even when you're not working.

What Happens When You Master Money Instead of Serving It

When you start treating money as a tool, rather than a measure of your worth, everything changes.

You stop making decisions out of fear of loss.

You stop chasing for the sake of chasing.

You stop working just to keep up a lifestyle that no longer makes you happy.

Instead, you:

Build wealth in a way that creates freedom, not just obligations.

Make choices based on your values, not just your income potential.

Design a life where money is a means to an end—not the end itself.

Because real wealth?

It is not just about how much you make.

It is about how much of yourself you get to keep in the process.

SECTION 3: **The Emotional Toll of Wealth— How Money Warps Identity, Relationships, and Reality**

No one tells you that money has a psychological weight. That beyond the math, beyond the accounts and investments, beyond the numbers you track and chase, there is a shift in how you see yourself and how the world sees you.

People think money will free them, and in some ways, it does. But it also rewires your brain, your relationships, your expectations, and your fears. It changes how you interact with power, how you perceive risk, and how you define yourself. It makes you question whether the people in your life are here for you or for what you can offer. It creates a quiet paranoia, a subtle alienation, a distortion of reality that can creep in without you noticing.

Because when you have money, you don't just have resources. You have influence. And the way that influence affects you? It is not always in your control.

The Psychological Weight of Money—Why Having More Changes You, Whether You Want It To or Not

At its core, money is power. And the human brain is not wired to hold power without consequence.

Psychologists have studied the effects of power for decades, and the findings are eerily consistent: power alters perception, reduces empathy, and distorts self-awareness. The more power someone has—financial, social, corporate—the harder it becomes for them to see the world through the eyes of others.

It is not intentional. It is not always malicious. It is simply human nature.

Studies have shown that wealthy individuals, even when they started from humble beginnings, are more likely to underestimate how difficult it is for others to achieve the same success. They begin to believe that their success was primarily a result of their own intelligence, discipline, and hard work—ignoring the systemic advantages, lucky breaks, and external factors that played a role.

And the danger?

Once you start believing that you alone are responsible for your success, you also start believing that people who struggle are responsible for their own failures.

You begin to lose touch. You begin to judge more than you understand.

And if you are not careful, you become insulated—so far removed from what struggle actually feels like that you forget how much of your own journey was shaped by timing, access, and privilege.

This is how money creates moral distance.

Not because people with money are inherently selfish, but because wealth separates you from the discomfort of struggle. If you are no longer experiencing hardship firsthand, your brain naturally stops accounting for it in others.

This is why wealthy people often say things like:

"Why don't they just work harder?"
"I pulled myself up, why can't they?"
"I started with nothing and figured it out—what's their excuse?"

Because money is not just a resource. It is a filter. It changes how you see effort, struggle, and fairness. And if you do not actively fight against that shift, you will wake up one day unable to recognize the person you used to be.

The Social Isolation of Wealth—Why More Money Often Means Fewer Real Relationships

When you have money, the world starts treating you differently.

It starts with small things—people deferring to you more, treating your opinions as more valuable simply because they come from someone who has "made it." Friends start assuming you can pick up the tab. Family members begin expecting help, as if your success was meant to be shared.

And at first, you don't mind.

But over time, you begin to wonder:

Would these people still be here if I lost everything?

Would they still respect me if I had nothing to offer?

Money distorts relationships because it creates an imbalance in power. Even when you try to downplay it, even when you insist that nothing has changed, it has.

Your friends who are still struggling may feel uncomfortable around you, even if they don't say it.
Your family may resent you, even as they ask for help.
Your business partners may respect you, but only as long as you remain valuable to them.

And the scariest part?

Once you reach a certain level of success, you can never be sure if new people in your life are drawn to you—or to what you represent.

This is why so many wealthy people feel lonelier than ever, even as they accumulate more.
This is why so many successful people become paranoid about trust.

This is why so many high-achievers wake up one day surrounded by people—but still feel completely alone.

Because wealth, if you are not careful, becomes a barrier instead of a bridge.

It separates you. It isolates you.

And unless you actively work against it, it will make you believe that you are better off alone.

The Fear of Losing What You've Built—Why the Richest People Are Often the Most Anxious

People assume that money eliminates fear. That once you hit a certain income level, once you have the house, the investments, the security, you will finally feel safe.

But the truth is, money does not erase fear. It often amplifies it.

Because the moment you have something to lose, you start living in fear of losing it.

The hustler mentality never truly leaves.
You keep pushing, keep working, keep expanding—not because you need to, but because stopping feels dangerous.

This is why millionaires still check their bank accounts obsessively.
This is why people with more money than they could ever spend still feel the need to chase more.
This is why people who have *made it* often feel more trapped than they did when they were broke.

Because once you build something, there is pressure to sustain it.
Once you create an identity around success, you feel like you can never afford to fail.

And so, instead of feeling safe, you feel responsible.

Responsible for maintaining your image.
Responsible for never slipping.
Responsible for making sure you do not return to where you started.

And this? This is why so many wealthy people are more stressed, more anxious, and more emotionally unstable than they were before they had money.

Because money does not solve your fears.

It magnifies them.

And unless you are intentional about how you manage that fear, you will live your entire life in a state of quiet paranoia.

The Antidote—How to Hold Wealth Without Letting It Break You

If you do not want money to consume you, you must treat it as a tool, not an identity.

That means:

> Surrounding yourself with people who knew you before money.

> Checking yourself before you become disconnected from reality.

> Making sure your success does not come at the cost of your peace.

> Using wealth to create freedom—not to build a prison of obligations and expectations.

Because the goal was never just to make money.

The goal was to build a life that feels rich in every way.

And if you lose sight of that?

Then no matter how much you accumulate, you will always feel like something is missing.

SECTION 4: **Wealth as a Living Thing—What Money Grows, Destroys, and Leaves Behind**

Money is alive. It is not static, not passive, not just numbers in a bank account or figures on a balance sheet. It breathes into every aspect of your life, shaping the way you think, the way you move, the way you relate to yourself and to others. It is a force—one that expands or contracts based on how you wield it, one that can be used to build something meaningful or to create destruction you never intended.

Most people assume money will solve their problems, that financial security will bring them peace, that once they reach a certain number, all of the tension they carry will dissolve into relief. But wealth does not work like that. It is not a finish line; it is a landscape that keeps shifting beneath you. It does not simply sit in your hands, waiting to be spent. It grows if you feed it, withers if you ignore it, and mutates if you let it control you.

Some people build wealth and use it to create impact, to open doors, to provide stability—not just for themselves but for the people and causes they care about. Others accumulate wealth only to find that it isolates them, that it breeds a paranoia they never expected, that it shifts them into a state of relentless protection, hoarding, and anxiety. Because the thing about money is that it does not just exist—it expands into every crevice of your life, for better or for worse. It amplifies whatever is already there, magnifying your best instincts or exposing your worst flaws.

If you are generous, wealth will make you a benefactor. If you are greedy, wealth will make you a hoarder. If you are insecure, wealth will make you paranoid. If you are obsessed with power, wealth will make you ruthless. If you are intentional, wealth will make you a builder. And if you are lost, wealth will make you more lost than ever before.

The question is not just how much money you make, but what kind of life your wealth is feeding.

Because whether you realize it or not, your money is shaping your future as much as your choices are.

When Wealth Becomes a Fortress Instead of a Bridge

The pursuit of financial success often begins as a way to create freedom, a means to provide security, a way to ensure that you and the people you love are never at the mercy of scarcity again. But there is a turning point that few people recognize until they have passed it—the moment when money stops being a gateway to more options and becomes something that isolates you from reality.

At first, wealth opens doors, expands your possibilities, gives you breathing room to make choices you never had before. But unchecked, it also builds walls. It changes the way you experience the world, the way people interact with you, the way you calculate risk. The higher you climb, the more removed you become, until one day, you are no longer living among people—you are looking down at them from a distance.

You stop feeling the urgency of financial struggle, and as a result, you forget what it was like to make decisions when survival was a factor. You lose touch with what it means to struggle with small choices, to weigh basic costs, to make sacrifices that once felt monumental. The numbers that used to mean something to you start to blur. A hundred dollars, a thousand, ten thousand—it does not carry the same weight anymore, and with that shift comes an unspoken separation from the world you once knew.

This is how wealth isolates.

Not because people with money intentionally detach, but because they no longer live with the same constraints, and over time, those constraints become impossible to imagine. They start giving advice that feels out of touch, making decisions that disregard the reality of the people they claim to help, moving through life in a way that is fundamentally disconnected from what struggle actually feels like.

And the scariest part? Most of them do not even notice that it has happened.

Because when you build a life that is insulated by money, you stop seeing the world through the same lens as everyone else.

You believe in hard work, because your hard work got you here—but you forget that not everyone has the same starting point. You believe in fairness, because you have made fair deals—but you forget that the system itself is not designed to be fair. You believe in meritocracy, because you worked your way up—but you forget that you were given opportunities that others were never even in the room to compete for.

If you do not actively fight against this detachment, wealth will put distance between you and the reality of the world. It will turn you into someone who speaks about struggle as if it is theoretical. It will make you more concerned with protecting what you have than with ensuring that what you have actually matters. It will make you believe that your comfort is the only thing worth defending.

And that? That is how money hollows you out.

The Wealth That Actually Means Something

If money was just money, it would be simple. It would be a resource, a tool, a neutral force that simply moves through hands and systems without affecting the people who hold it. But money is not just money. It is power, it is opportunity, it is influence, and it is a reflection of what you value.

You can use it to build, to create, to support, to expand. Or you can use it to hoard, to isolate, to dominate, to control. The way you handle wealth is a direct statement about what kind of person you are.

Some people build generational wealth only to pass down money without wisdom, leaving their children with riches but no understanding of how to hold it, leading them into cycles of excess, entitlement, or waste. Others create wealth and use it to open doors, ensuring that the people around them have not just resources, but the ability to sustain them. Some use money to buy freedom. Others use money to create cages, wrapped in gold but isolating all the same.

What kind of wealth are you building?

Because money in itself means nothing.

A million dollars, ten million, a hundred million—none of it matters if it does not give you a life that actually feels worth living.

If you are working only to accumulate, if you are grinding without stopping, if you are so focused on making more that you never pause to ask what you are making it for, then you are not wealthy.

You are just a highly paid prisoner.

The only wealth that matters is the kind that lets you live on your own terms.

That means defining your own version of success.
That means deciding how much is enough before you get there.
That means making sure that your money is a tool—not an identity.

Because at the end of your life, you will not care about your net worth.

You will care about whether or not you spent your days chasing numbers that did not matter, or building something that did.

Toolkit: How to Build a Healthy Relationship with Money and Add Value to Your Wealth

Money is not just about numbers. It is about how you engage with it, how it moves through your life, and what it represents to you. Most people either fear money, obsess over it, or ignore it altogether. But the healthiest relationship with wealth is one of intention, not reaction.

This toolkit is designed to help you redefine your connection to money, use it as a tool rather than a burden, and ensure that your wealth enhances your life rather than controls it.

Step 1: Redefine What Money Means to You

Money is not just income or numbers on a statement. It is a mirror reflecting your values, fears, ambitions, and beliefs about self-worth. To build a healthy relationship with it, you must rewrite the subconscious script you have been following.

Actionable Exercise:

Sit down with a journal and answer the following:

- What was I taught about money growing up? (Was it a source of stress? A measure of success? A tool? A weapon?)
- What emotions come up when I think about money? (Anxiety? Guilt? Power? Relief?)
- Do I view money as something I chase, control, or attract?
- How do I behave when I have more than enough vs. when I have less?
- If money were a person, what kind of relationship would I have with it? Am I neglectful, controlling, afraid, or secure?

Understanding your emotional blueprint with money is critical. If you do not actively reframe it, you will continue to repeat unconscious financial patterns.

Step 2: Define What "Enough" Looks Like

If you do not define "enough," you will **never reach it.** The goalpost will always move. You will always think **you need more.**

Most people **do not have a real number** for what financial stability, freedom, or abundance means to them. Without one, they fall into **chronic chasing mode.**

Actionable Exercise:

▶ **Identify your baseline needs.** Calculate the exact amount you need per month to cover your essentials.

▶ **Define your financial freedom number.** How much would you need per year to live life on your own terms?

▶ **Decide on your legacy amount.** If you were to leave behind wealth, what would it be used for? Who would it serve?

By setting tangible numbers, you stop chasing money as an abstract idea and start using it with purpose.

Step 3: Use Money as a Tool, Not a Trap

Money should be working for you, not the other way around. Too many people trade their time and energy indefinitely for money without creating a system that allows wealth to generate itself.

Actionable Steps to Make Money Work for You:

1. Create a Wealth Flowchart. Write down how money currently flows into and out of your life. If all your income depends on

active work, you are trapped in an endless loop. Find ways to redirect some of your money into systems that grow passively.

2. Build an "Autopilot" Account System. Your money should be organized into automatic buckets—one for spending, one for saving, one for investing, and one for giving. Every dollar that comes in should have a purpose before it touches your hands.

3. Adopt the "Buy Once, Cry Once" Mentality. Stop buying cheap things that break or depreciate quickly. Invest in quality over quantity. Spend more on things that create efficiency, last longer, and save time.

4. Detach Your Self-Worth from Your Net Worth. Your bank account should not dictate your confidence. Money is a resource, not a personality trait. If you build your identity on your wealth, you will live in fear of losing it.

Step 4: Balance Wealth With Impact

Wealth is most powerful when it is shared, reinvested, and used with intention. Many people reach financial success only to isolate themselves, hoard their earnings, or spend without meaning. The healthiest relationship with money is one where it benefits not just you, but others as well.

Actionable Strategies for Purposeful Wealth:

▶ Adopt a "Give and Grow" Approach. Allocate a percentage of your income to something bigger than yourself. Whether it is philanthropy, supporting loved ones, or investing in community projects, money that circulates with intention grows in value.

▶ Redefine Investment Beyond Profits. Invest in experiences, relationships, and skill-building. The best returns are often not financial, but in life enrichment.

▶ Protect Your Wealth From Your Own Ego. Just because you can buy it does not mean you should. Spend in ways that reflect your values, not just your impulses.

Step 5: Design a Life Where Money Supports You, Not Controls You

The healthiest relationship with money is one where it is an asset, not a source of anxiety. You should be able to walk away from your work and still have a fulfilling life.

Most people do not build their life this way. They work endlessly, accumulate wealth, but have no idea how to enjoy it.

How to Build a Money-Managed Life That Feels Balanced:

▶ Create a "Money-Free" Identity. Who are you outside of your work and financial achievements? If all your wealth disappeared tomorrow, what would still make your life meaningful?

▶ Schedule Money-Free Days. Regularly have days where you do not check accounts, think about investments, or make financial decisions. This keeps money from being a constant mental burden.

▶ Make Sure Your Hustle Ends Somewhere. Do not create a lifestyle that requires you to hustle indefinitely. Wealth should be used to buy time, not just more status.

Because at the end of the day, money should never be the goal.

The goal is to have a life that feels rich, whether or not your accounts are full.

Final Takeaway: The Currency of a Meaningful Life

If you do not redefine your relationship with money, it will define you.

If you do not decide how much is enough, you will chase endlessly.
If you do not structure wealth to serve your life, it will become your life.
If you do not use your money with intention, you will end up consumed by what it can buy instead of what it can create.

A rich life is not about a number.

It is about the ability to wake up every day and know that your time, your values, and your energy are yours to manage.

It is about freedom—not from work, but from the need to constantly prove yourself through accumulation.

Because in the end, the real currency of life is not just money.

It is time.
It is presence.
It is meaning.

And if your wealth does not allow you to live more deeply, love more fully, and be more present in the life you are building, then what is it really worth?

JOURNEY JOTS

*Quick, thoughtful notes that document milestones,
insights, and personal growth*

JOURNEY JOTS

Quick, thoughtful notes that document milestones, insights, and personal growth

JOURNEY JOTS

*Quick, thoughtful notes that document milestones,
insights, and personal growth*

_____

_____

_____

_____

_____

_____

_____

_____

_____

_____

_____

_____

_____

_____

_____

_____

_____

_____

CHAPTER

08

Self-Care is Not Just Bubble Baths

The modern self-care movement has been packaged and sold like a luxury product.

It looks like soft lighting, skincare routines, overpriced candles, and the occasional yoga retreat. It is indulgent, aesthetic, a break from the chaos of daily life.

And yet—so many people are still burnt out.

Because what's marketed as self-care is often just temporary relief from the exhaustion of a life that is fundamentally unsustainable.

Self-care is not a break from the stress you can't escape.
Self-care is redesigning your life so that you don't need to constantly escape from it.

If your version of self-care is just treating the symptoms of burnout, then it is not care—it is a coping mechanism.

Real self-care? It's not about adding bubble baths.
It's about removing what is draining you in the first place.

SECTION 1: The False Cure—Why Most Self-Care Isn't Actually Self-Care

If self-care is only something you do when you're already drained, it's not self-care—it's damage control.

That's the part people don't talk about.

They tell you to relax, to unwind, to "take a break." They sell you bath salts and meditation apps like they're cures for exhaustion, like a scented candle can reverse months—maybe years—of chronic stress, overcommitment, and emotional depletion.

But if you need a recovery plan just to survive your own life, what does that say about the life you're living?

The real problem isn't that people aren't doing enough self-care.
The problem is that they are building lives that require constant recovery.

Because most of what we call self-care isn't about care at all.
It's about patching up the symptoms of a broken system.

And that's why so many people still feel exhausted, burned out, and stuck—even when they are "taking care of themselves."

Because real self-care isn't about soothing the damage.

It's about removing the things that are causing the damage in the first place.

The Self-Care That Changes Nothing

It's easy to fall into the illusion of self-care.

To convince yourself that you're prioritizing your well-being because you're checking off all the right boxes.

> You take breaks.

> You exercise.

> You unplug from work on weekends.

> You do all the things you're supposed to do.

But if you're doing all of that and still feel like you're barely holding yourself together, then what you are doing isn't self-care.

It's maintenance.

It's what you do to keep functioning despite the fact that something in your life is deeply misaligned.

And that's why the relief never lasts.

Because you are treating the symptoms instead of fixing the cause.

If your "self-care" doesn't create actual change, then it is just a way to make exhaustion feel slightly more tolerable.

And that? That is not self-care. That is survival.

The Things That Pretend to Be Self-Care But Aren't

Most people don't realize that half of the things they call self-care are actually coping mechanisms for avoidable stress.

> If your job is destroying your mental health, quitting is self-care—not a vacation.

> If your relationships are draining you, setting boundaries is self-care—not venting about it over brunch.

> If you are overwhelmed, removing commitments is self-care—not just trying to "manage stress" better.

But those things require change.

And change is uncomfortable.

So instead, we settle for temporary relief.

We tell ourselves that if we just recharge enough, we'll be able to keep pushing.

But if your life is so exhausting that you need to constantly recharge, then the problem is not a lack of self-care.

The problem is that you are not designing a sustainable life to begin with.

The Hardest Kind of Self-Care—The One That Actually Works

Real self-care? It's not glamorous.

It does not fit neatly into an Instagram post. It does not always feel relaxing.
In fact, the most effective self-care is often the most uncomfortable.

Because real self-care is:

> Confronting the habits that are making you miserable.

> Saying no to things that no longer serve you—even when it disappoints people.

> Creating a schedule that actually allows for rest—instead of just recovering when you crash.

> Removing yourself from places where you are only valued for what you can give.

And that?

That is harder than lighting a candle and taking a bath.

Because real self-care requires boundaries. Choices. Change.

And that is why most people don't do it.

Because comfort is easier than correction.

Because it is easier to recover from a toxic cycle than it is to break it.

And because if we actually practiced real self-care, we would have to give up the things that are secretly keeping us stuck.

What Happens When You Stop Doing Self-Care Wrong

When you start practicing real self-care—the kind that actually transforms your life—everything shifts.

You no longer feel like you are constantly on the edge of burnout.
You no longer have to escape your own schedule just to feel okay.
You no longer rely on small bursts of relaxation to survive the chaos.

Because you are no longer living in chaos to begin with.

And the best part?

You don't have to keep fixing yourself every weekend just to make it through the next workweek.

Because when self-care is built into the structure of your life—not just added on top of the stress—you stop needing to recover all the time.

And that?

That is what real self-care is supposed to feel like.

SECTION 2: **The Architecture of a Sustainable Life**

Most people approach self-care like damage control. They push themselves to the edge of burnout, then try to recover just enough to keep going.

But self-care was never supposed to be a desperate attempt to refill an empty tank.

It was supposed to be the foundation of how you structure your life.

Not something you do in response to exhaustion.
Something you do to prevent exhaustion from happening in the first place.

This section is about how to stop treating self-care like a rescue plan—and start treating it like the architecture of a life you don't have to recover from.

The Problem with "Adding" Self-Care Instead of Designing Around It

The way most people approach self-care is reactionary.

They recognize they are exhausted, so they try to add things that will make them feel better.
They squeeze in exercise, meditation, a hobby—but they do not remove the things that are draining them.

So instead of self-care feeling like a natural part of their life, it feels like another obligation on an already overwhelming list.

And that is why it never works.

Because real self-care is not about adding.

It is about redesigning.

It is about looking at your entire life—your work, your relationships, your responsibilities—and asking:

> What in my life is sustainable?

> What in my life is costing me more energy than it gives me?

> Where am I placing self-care at the bottom of the list instead of designing my life around it?

Because you do not "make time" for self-care.

You build your life so that time for yourself is non-negotiable.

How to Build a Life That Doesn't Require Constant Recovery

If you are tired of living in cycles of burnout and recovery, you need to stop fitting self-care into a broken system.

You need to rebuild the system.

Here's how.

1. Design Your Life for Recovery Before You Need It

Most people don't think about self-care until they are already running on fumes.

They wait until they are exhausted, overwhelmed, mentally and physically drained—and then they try to fix it.

But by then? It's already too late.

A well-designed life does not require you to be on the brink of collapse before you rest.

So instead of waiting until you are drained, schedule recovery into your life as if it is part of your job.

> Rest is not what you do when you've "earned" it. It is what allows you to keep showing up fully.

> Breaks are not a sign of weakness. They are a strategy for longevity.

> Recovery is not an occasional indulgence. It is a requirement for sustained success.

If you do not proactively build rest into your schedule, you will be forced to take it in ways that are far more painful, whether through illness, mental breakdown, or burnout so severe it takes months or years to recover from.

2. Stop Overextending Yourself for Things That Don't Matter

One of the biggest energy leaks in most people's lives is obligation.

They say yes to things they don't want to do.
They take on responsibilities that are not theirs to carry.
They spread themselves so thin that there is nothing left for themselves.

And then, when they finally have time for self-care, they are too drained to even enjoy it.

This is why self-care starts with cutting, not adding.

> Cut the social obligations that exhaust you.

> Cut the relationships that drain more than they give.

> Cut the idea that your time belongs to anyone but you.

Because it does not matter how much self-care you add if you do not remove the things that are taking too much from you.

3. Build a Life That Aligns With Your Natural Energy Cycles

The modern world is built for productivity, not sustainability.

It expects you to perform at the same level every day, no matter what your body, mind, or emotions are experiencing.

But real self-care is about working with yourself, not against yourself.

> If you are most creative in the mornings, schedule your deep work then.

> If you crash in the afternoons, stop forcing yourself to be productive when your brain is offline.

> If your weekends are your time to recharge, stop filling them with obligations.

Your energy is not a constant.

And if you do not structure your life to respect that reality, you will always feel like you are failing—not because you are, but because you are working against your natural rhythms instead of with them.

4. Redefine Success—Because If You're Burned Out, You're Not Winning

Too many people think success means sacrificing everything in the short term for some distant, future reward.

They convince themselves that once they hit a certain income, build their career, achieve their goal—then they will finally have time to enjoy their life.

But what if that never happens?

What if you reach your goal only to realize you have no energy left to enjoy it?

What if you build success at the cost of your health, your relationships, your peace?

If your version of success requires you to burn yourself to the ground to achieve it, then you are not winning.

Because real success is not just what you build.

It is how much of yourself you still have left when you get there.

The Self-Care That Actually Works—A Blueprint for Sustainability

If you want a life that does not require you to constantly recover from it, here's what you do:

> Stop structuring your schedule around productivity and start structuring it around energy management.
>
> Stop saying yes to things that drain you just because you feel obligated.
>
> Stop living for a future where you'll "finally have time" and start making space now.
>
> Stop treating self-care as a luxury and start treating it as the foundation of everything else.

Because if you do not take care of yourself now, you will spend your entire life trying to recover from the damage.

And by then?

You may not get the time back.

SECTION 3: The Memory of Who You Were— Why Self-Care is a Return, Not an Escape

There was a time before exhaustion.

A time before you built a life that required you to be on all the time, before your worth became tangled up in how much you could accomplish, how much you could endure, how much you could prove. There was a time when you existed purely in the moment—when your laughter wasn't weighed down by deadlines, when your body wasn't always bracing for the next thing, when your mind didn't feel like it was constantly running a marathon with no finish line.

You did not enter this world like this—this tired, stretched-thin, never-enough version of yourself. You became this way.

And if you became this way, that means you can also become something else.

But to do that, you have to stop looking at self-care as an escape and start seeing it for what it really is—a return.

Because real self-care isn't about stepping away from your life for a moment of relief. It's about stepping back into yourself, into the version of you that existed before you started sacrificing your peace for productivity, before you started carrying burdens that were never yours to hold.

The Version of You That Still Exists Beneath the Burnout

If you were to strip away all the expectations—if, for one moment, you stopped being the person you've trained yourself to be, the one who always has an answer, always has a plan, always has it together—who would be left?

Would you recognize yourself?

Would you still know how to move through the world without urgency, without always anticipating the next thing, without constantly trying to justify your own existence?

For many, the answer is no.

Because the longer you live in service of everything outside of yourself— your job, your obligations, the expectations placed on you by people who do not have to live with the consequences of your exhaustion—the further you drift from the part of you that once knew how to just be.

At some point, you started believing that survival required sacrifice. That growing up meant giving up the version of you who didn't need a reason to rest, to create, to wander, to simply exist without being useful. You buried that part of yourself under responsibilities, under the weight of expectations, under the belief that a good life is an earned life, that peace must be purchased with productivity.

But she is still there.

The version of you that existed before the burnout, before the exhaustion, before you started measuring your worth by how much of yourself you could give away—she is still waiting for you.

And self-care?

Self-care is not about pampering the version of you that is drowning in responsibility.

Self-care is about rescuing the version of you that should have never been abandoned.

The Emotional Weight of Forgetting Yourself

It is easy to think of exhaustion as just a physical depletion. A problem that can be solved with rest, with sleep, with a few days off. But true exhaustion—the kind that makes you feel like you are disappearing inside your own life—is not just about how much you do. It is about how much of yourself you have lost in the process.

Because when you spend too long prioritizing everything and everyone else, you do not just feel tired. You feel unrecognizable.

It happens so subtly that you do not even notice the shift. One day, you stop doing the things that once made you feel alive—not because you don't love them anymore, but because there are more important things to do. You tell yourself you will get back to them later, when things calm down, when there's more time, when you are less overwhelmed.

But time keeps moving. And before you realize it, you have become a person who only exists inside their responsibilities. You have become someone whose identity is built entirely on what you can provide, on what you can accomplish, on what you can endure.

And deep down, you feel it.

That empty space inside of you, the one that cannot be filled with more work, more achievements, more obligations. The part of you that aches for something you cannot name, because you do not even remember what is missing—only that something is.

And so, you distract yourself. You keep moving. You keep proving. You keep adding more to your plate, convincing yourself that if you just get through this next thing, if you just push a little harder, everything will settle, and you will finally feel like yourself again.

But what if the version of you that you are waiting to return to no longer exists?

What if you have gone so long without being her that you have to actively bring her back?

Relearning the Language of Self—How to Reconnect with the Person You Lost

If you have spent years, maybe decades, living in a state of constant doing, you will not simply wake up one day and remember how to be.

You will have to relearn yourself.

You will have to sit in silence without the need to fill it with a task.
You will have to do things for joy without tying them to an outcome.
You will have to rebuild your own rhythm, not the one the world demands of you.

And that? That will feel uncomfortable.

Because there is a grief in remembering the parts of yourself that you abandoned. There is a sadness in realizing how long you have lived without them, in seeing how much time has passed since you last let yourself move without urgency, breathe without guilt, exist without justification.

But this is the work.

The work is not just resting.
The work is learning how to feel safe in stillness again.
The work is choosing yourself, not just in fleeting moments of rebellion, but as a permanent and unwavering act of self-respect.

The work is allowing yourself to take up space in your own life.

The Self-Care That Actually Brings You Back

Real self-care is not an escape. It is a homecoming.

And homecoming is not about making time for yourself once in a while. It is not about penciling in an hour of self-care in between responsibilities. It is about returning to the person you were before the world convinced you that she had to be left behind.

It is about remembering what lights you up.
It is about choosing things because they feel right, not because they are productive.
It is about no longer treating yourself as an afterthought in your own story.

And the next time you feel exhausted, the next time you feel like you are disappearing, the next time you feel like you need a break just to keep surviving—ask yourself if you are actually exhausted, or if you are just homesick for yourself.

Because self-care is not a break from life.

Self-care is the act of reclaiming it.

SECTION 4: **What If I Never Left?—A Restful Awakening (A DEEP Reflection)**

I lay there with her, my subconscious, in the wreckage of everything I had ignored. The vault was empty, not because I had nothing left to give, but because I had given so much that I no longer knew how to receive. I had spent years running a one-way transaction—depositing love, care, time, pieces of myself into others, never stopping to wonder if I had enough left for me. I had been so consumed with making sure everyone else had what they needed that I never asked what I needed. And now, here I was. Empty. Dry. Angry.

Angry, because I had never expected it to come to this. Angry, because I had always believed that love, when given freely, multiplies. And it had, in some ways. But I was the one who had been left out of the equation. I had spent so much time ensuring that no one in my life ever felt forgotten, unseen, unloved—but I had forgotten, unseen, and unloved myself.

Lying there at rock bottom, I realized the real problem wasn't that I had nothing left to give. The problem was that I had never stopped long enough to ask if I had ever given anything to myself. I had never walked into my own vault. Never opened it for myself. Never stood there with a gift, a moment of care, an ounce of the love I so easily poured into others.

I had been so convinced that I was awake, so certain that I was present and engaged in life, but I wasn't. I had been running on autopilot, performing generosity out of habit, so asleep in my own exhaustion that I didn't even recognize that I needed saving.

But I saw it now.

I saw the layers of self-neglect I had justified as kindness. I saw the way I had ignored my own depletion in the name of being strong. I saw how I had confused martyrdom for love, how I had mistaken sacrifice for selflessness. And in that moment, I realized that giving is only beautiful when it is sustainable.

I did not want to be bitter. I did not want to be resentful. I did not want to keep holding this anger like it was a punishment for the world when really, it was a message from myself.

And so, I did the only thing I could do. I met myself where I was.

I did not fight my exhaustion. I did not demand an instant recovery. I did not try to force myself into healing faster than my soul was ready.

Instead, I did what I had done for so many others—I stood at my own vault, and I gave.

I gave myself patience. I gave myself softness. I gave myself the right to be tired without guilt, to rest without justification, to take without feeling like I owed the world an explanation. I gave myself permission to exist, not just as a giver, but as someone worthy of receiving.

And in that act, in that simple, quiet moment of choosing myself—not out of selfishness, but out of necessity—I felt something shift. It was not loud. It was not a grand revelation. It was just a whisper, a small flicker of something that had been buried for too long.

I was still here.

I had never left. I had just gone quiet, waiting, watching, protecting myself in the only way I knew how. My subconscious had shut down not because I was broken, but because I needed rest. And now, slowly, gently, I was waking up again.

This time, not to continue the cycle. Not to run myself into the ground in the name of love. Not to overextend, over-give, over-sacrifice. But to finally exist in my own life the way I had always wished others would exist in theirs—with care, with attention, with deep, unwavering compassion.

The kind of compassion I had always given so freely.

And for the first time, I gave it to myself.

Toolkit: How to Rebuild Yourself Through Real Self-Care

Self-care is not a retreat. It is not a moment of escape. It is not a surface-level indulgence to temporarily ease the discomfort of a life that is exhausting you.

Self-care is the foundation upon which you build everything else. It is how you return to yourself, how you unlearn the belief that your worth is measured by your exhaustion, how you wake up from the autopilot existence you have been surviving in.

This toolkit is not just a list of things to do—it is a roadmap back to yourself.

These are the practical, psychological, and emotional tools to help you shift from self-neglect to self-preservation, from running on empty to creating a life that does not require you to constantly recover from it.

This is where your return begins.

Step 1: Conduct a Full-Life Audit—Where Have You Been Overdrawing Yourself?

You cannot rebuild what you do not assess.

The first step in reclaiming yourself is to figure out where you have been over-giving, over-functioning, over-extending.

Take out a notebook and go through these categories:

- Your energy—Where is it going every day? Who or what is taking the most from you?
- Your time—Are you spending it on things that nourish you or just things that drain you?

- Your boundaries—Do you have any? Do you enforce them?
- Your emotional load—How much of what you carry actually belongs to you?

Actionable Task:

For one full day, track everything that takes your energy, your attention, your mental space. Every conversation, every obligation, every moment of invisible labor. Write it all down.

At the end of the day, highlight everything that felt like a demand rather than a choice. That is where you start.

Step 2: Rewrite Your Definition of Rest—What Does Real Self-Care Look Like for You?

Most people only know how to rest when they have earned it. They only allow themselves a break when they have worked themselves to exhaustion, when their body forces them to slow down, when they have nothing left to give.

But self-care should not be a desperate attempt to recover from burnout. It should be a built-in part of your life.

Actionable Task:

Sit with these questions and write down your answers:

1. What does real rest look like for me?
2. If I were designing a life where I never felt constantly exhausted, what would it include?
3. What kinds of rest actually recharge me (mental, emotional, physical, creative)?
4. What is one way I can integrate rest into my life before I hit a breaking point?

Then, schedule it. Right now. Not for when you have time. Not for when everything else is handled. Make it non-negotiable.

Because if you do not prioritize your well-being, no one else will.

Step 3: Withdraw from the Emotional Overdraft— Stop Giving What You No Longer Have

If you are constantly exhausted, constantly drained, constantly feeling like you have nothing left to give, you are operating in an emotional deficit.

And if you do not stop, you will go bankrupt.

It is time to reassess where your emotional energy is going and cut back where necessary.

Actionable Task:

1. Make a list of people, responsibilities, and habits that drain you. Be brutally honest.
2. Ask yourself: *If I continue to give this much to these things, where will I be a year from now?*
3. Choose one area where you immediately reduce access. Not later. Not when you have time. Right now.

You are allowed to give less to things that do not pour back into you. You are allowed to choose yourself over obligation.

This is not selfish. This is survival.

Step 4: Practice Receiving Without Guilt

Some people only know how to give. They have built their entire identity around being the one who shows up, who supports, who never asks for anything in return. And even when they are drowning, they refuse to reach for help because they have spent their entire lives believing that their worth is in what they offer, not in who they are.

This needs to stop.

Actionable Task:

1. Ask for help in one small way this week. It does not matter what it is—something simple, something easy. Just get in the practice of receiving.
2. Say yes when someone offers you something. A favor, support, kindness—accept it.
3. Notice how you feel when you do. If guilt creeps in, if discomfort rises, acknowledge it, but do not let it control you.

You are allowed to take up space.

You are allowed to let people pour into you, just as you have poured into them.

Step 5: Redesign Your Daily Life to Support You—Not Just Others

Most people structure their days around obligations, not around well-being.

They design their lives based on what other people need from them, what work demands of them, what society expects of them. But they never stop to ask if their life is actually working for them.

It is time to rebuild.

Actionable Task:

1. Design a "Bare Minimum Day" for yourself. What would your life look like if you only did what was absolutely necessary?
2. Identify 3 things you do every day that deplete you. Can they be eliminated? Delegated? Reduced?

3. Create a boundary that protects your personal time. Whether it is an hour of silence, an evening to yourself, or a morning routine that is yours alone—make it untouchable.

A life that does not drain you is a life that does not need constant escape.

And if you do not actively create that life, exhaustion will always be waiting for you.

Step 6: Make Rest a Non-Negotiable Ritual, Not a Last Resort

The biggest mistake people make with self-care is treating it like a luxury. They see it as something extra, something optional, something that can wait. But self-care is not a reward for hard work.

It is the foundation that makes hard work possible.

If you do not start treating rest as an essential, unbreakable part of your life, you will always be running on fumes.

Actionable Task:

1. Create a daily ritual that forces you to slow down. Not a "when I have time" activity. A non-negotiable act of self-preservation.
2. Stop waiting for exhaustion to rest. Build it into your routine, just like eating, just like breathing.
3. Normalize rest as a sign of strength, not weakness. When you take care of yourself, you are not slacking—you are securing your longevity.

Because if you do not give yourself permission to rest, your body will force you to. And by then, it will not be a choice. It will be a consequence.

The Final Takeaway: You Are Allowed to Exist Outside of What You Do for Others

If you take nothing else from this toolkit, take this:

You are not required to run yourself into the ground just to prove you are worthy.

You are not obligated to be everything for everyone while abandoning yourself.

You are not defined by how much you produce, how much you sacrifice, how much you endure.

You just are.

And you deserve to care for yourself simply because you exist.

Not when you are exhausted.
Not when you have earned it.
Not when everything else is done.

Now.

Because the moment you stop treating self-care as something you *fit into your life* and start treating it as the thing that makes your life livable—

That is the moment everything changes.

JOURNEY JOTS

Quick, thoughtful notes that document milestones, insights, and personal growth

JOURNEY JOTS

Quick, thoughtful notes that document milestones,
insights, and personal growth

JOURNEY JOTS

Quick, thoughtful notes that document milestones, insights, and personal growth

CHAPTER

09

The Life Detox—A One-Day Reset for a Lifetime Shift

SECTION 1: **The Detox**

If you could step outside your life for just one day—no obligations, no distractions, no outside noise—what would you see?

Would you be proud of how your time is spent?
Would you feel in control of your energy?
Would your choices actually align with the life you say you want?

Most people never pause long enough to ask. They wake up, follow their routines, respond to the world's demands, and never stop to evaluate whether their life is even working for them.

This is why we detox.

Not as an escape.
Not as a self-indulgent break.
But as a full reset.

Because you cannot manage what you do not examine.

And if you want a life that actually feels manageable, fulfilling, and aligned, you have to clear out everything that is keeping you stuck.

This chapter is your blueprint for a complete life detox—a single day to assess, purge, and rebuild.

One day.
One reset.
A permanent shift.

Step 1: The Mental Detox—Clearing Out the Invisible Weight

Before you detox anything external, you must clear your mind.

Because most of your exhaustion? It is not physical.
It is the mental load.

You are carrying thoughts that do not belong to you.
You are running through mental checklists before you even get out of bed.
You are holding onto worries, expectations, and obligations that are not even yours to solve.

Today, you empty them out.

How to Detox Your Mind:

> Brain dump every unfinished thought. Every worry, every to-do, every lingering responsibility—get it out of your head and onto paper.

> Challenge the "rules" you've been living by. Who told you that you have to be everything for everyone at all times? Who convinced you that you are failing if you need a break?

> Decide what thoughts deserve space in your life. If a belief is keeping you exhausted, it does not belong. If a worry is outside of your control, it does not deserve your time.

Because if your mind is constantly full, you will never have room for clarity.

Step 2: The Relationship Detox—Redefining Access to Your Energy

You cannot always choose who is in your life.

But you can choose how you engage with them.

If you are a parent, a caregiver, or someone with non-negotiable responsibilities, this is not about cutting people out.

It is about adjusting the flow of energy.

> If you are always emotionally available to everyone but yourself, that is a drain.

> If you are always responding immediately to everyone's needs without considering your own, that is unsustainable.

> If you never get even ten minutes to be with your own thoughts, that is a warning sign.

How to Detox Your Relationships Without Abandoning Your Responsibilities:

> Shift your role from constant giver to conscious giver. You do not need to be everything, all the time, to everyone.

> Create pockets of time that are untouchable. Even if you can't disappear for a full detox day, you can designate 30 minutes where you do not answer to anyone.

> Teach people to wait. If you are always available, people will always expect you to be. It is okay for people to learn that you have limits, too.

Because you are allowed to be a full human being—not just a resource for others.

Step 3: The Physical Detox—Creating an Environment That Supports You

Your space is a reflection of your mind.

If it is cluttered, chaotic, and full of things that make you feel overwhelmed or obligated, that energy will follow you.

Today, you reclaim your environment.

How to Detox Your Space Without Disrupting Your Household:

> Eliminate the objects that carry emotional weight. The clothes you keep but never wear, the items tied to an old version of yourself—if it does not bring value, it does not belong.

> Simplify your daily surroundings. If your mornings are stressful, redesign your space so that they feel effortless. If your evenings feel rushed, create areas that invite calm instead of chaos.

> Create a space in your home that belongs entirely to you. Even if it is just a chair, a corner, a desk—a place where you can breathe without interruption.

Because your home should not just be a place where you manage life.

It should be a place where you feel at home in yourself.

Step 4: The Time Detox—Reclaiming Your Schedule From the Things That Waste It

Most of your exhaustion is not from doing too much.

It is from doing too much of what does not matter.

If you looked at your calendar today, would it reflect your priorities, or someone else's?

How to Detox Your Schedule Without Neglecting Your Responsibilities:

> Identify the obligations you inherited by default. If it does not align with where you are going, it is time to let it go.

> Reclaim your time in small, deliberate ways. If a full day off is not an option, start with an hour, a morning, an evening that is yours.

> Create structured flexibility. Build in space where nothing is scheduled—so that rest is not something you "fit in," but something that is already accounted for.

Because if your time is always being stolen by external demands, you will never have enough of it to build a life that feels manageable.

The Release—What Happens When You Detox Your Life

At the end of this detox, something happens.

Your mind feels like it has space again.
Your body feels lighter, because it is no longer carrying invisible weight.
Your time belongs to you again.

And the best part?

You finally understand that a manageable life is not something you stumble into.

It is something you create.

And today?

Today is the first time in a long time that you feel like you are actually in control of your own life.

SECTION 2: **The Detox Checklist—A Step-by-Step Guide to Reset Your Life**

Most people never stop long enough to question the weight they carry. They assume exhaustion is normal, that stress is the price of being an adult, that feeling behind is just part of life. They don't ask *Why does my life feel like this?* Instead, they assume they need to be more disciplined, more efficient, better at handling it all.

But what if the problem isn't that you need to handle more? What if the real issue is that you are handling things that were never meant for you?

Most people do not need to be *more productive*. They need to be *less burdened*. They do not need better time management. They need *better life management.*

This is the moment where you stop reacting to the chaos and start redesigning your existence. This is where you put everything in your life under a microscope and decide what stays and what goes. This is not about taking a break so you can return to the same exhausting cycle. This is about making sure that cycle never starts again.

A life detox is not about pausing. It is about eliminating every unnecessary, unaligned, and energy-draining aspect of your life so that you don't have to keep recovering from your own schedule. You will not just feel better after this. You will not just feel lighter. You will have rewired the structure of your days, your priorities, and your future.

If you do this right, there will be no going back.

The Mental Purge

Your brain is running a program it did not write. Every thought, every assumption, every reaction—so many of them are inherited, absorbed, and conditioned into you from childhood, from culture, from experiences that have long since expired. And yet, they are still running. You are still acting based on beliefs that may not even belong to you.

If you do not stop and audit these thoughts, they will continue to dictate the way you move through life. They will continue to decide for you. They will continue to *manage you*, instead of the other way around.

The first step of this detox is a full excavation of your thoughts. Sit down with a notebook and dump out every worry, fear, expectation, obligation, and lingering thought that has been taking up space in your head. Look at what you wrote. See how much of your mental energy is being spent on things you cannot control. See how much of your bandwidth is being drained by other people's problems, by things you have no intention of acting on, by thoughts that serve no purpose other than to exhaust you.

Now, ask yourself which of these thoughts are useful and which are just noise. You will find that most of what you carry in your head is clutter— unfinished loops, pointless worries, outdated narratives about who you are and what you are supposed to be.

Delete them. Write them down, cross them out, tear them up. If a thought does not serve you, it does not belong.

This is not a feel-good exercise. This is a mental exorcism. If you want to reclaim your clarity, you must first get rid of everything that is muddying your thinking. If a thought is weighing on you and you cannot solve it today, it is not your problem right now. Let it go. You will be shocked by how much mental capacity you regain once you stop carrying the thoughts that were never meant to stay.

The Relationship Purge

Who you give your energy to is one of the most important decisions of your life. But most people do not choose their relationships. They inherit them. They default into them. They continue them out of habit.

Not everyone deserves access to you. Not everyone should be allowed to shape your emotions, influence your self-worth, or dictate how you spend your time. But if you never stop to evaluate who is in your life, you will find yourself emotionally bankrupt—overdrawn by people who take more than they give, who drain more than they replenish, who expect more than they offer.

Take an inventory. Make a list of the people you interact with the most. Do not categorize them as *good* or *bad*. Simply assess them based on how you feel after engaging with them. Do you feel lighter or heavier? Do you feel supported or drained? Do you feel more like yourself, or do you feel like you have to perform for them?

You do not need to cut people off in a dramatic fashion. But you do need to reallocate your energy. Some people should no longer have unrestricted access to your mind, your emotions, and your time. Adjust accordingly. Spend less time where you feel exhausted. Spend more time where you feel seen and valued. And for those who make you feel consistently worse after engaging with them? Let them fade. Your energy is too precious to waste on people who do not treat it with care.

The Physical Purge

Look around your home. Look at everything you own. Do you even know why you are keeping most of it?

Objects carry mental weight. They are not just things—they are reminders. Of who you used to be. Of people you no longer speak to. Of goals you never achieved. Of past versions of yourself you are still holding onto.

Go through every room, every closet, every drawer. If it does not serve you, if it does not add value to your current life, if it does not actively contribute to the person you are becoming—it goes. No second-guessing. No *"but I might need this someday"*. If you have not used it, worn it, or thought about it in the last year, it is not serving you.

This is not minimalism for the sake of minimalism. This is about reclaiming your space as a place that works for you, not a storage unit for the past.

The moment you eliminate the excess, you will breathe differently. Your environment is an extension of your mind, and when you strip away what is unnecessary, your thoughts become clearer.

The Time Purge

Time is your most valuable, non-renewable resource. Yet, most people spend it as if they have an infinite supply.

Go through your schedule. Every meeting, every obligation, every "yes" that you agreed to without thinking. Ask yourself: *Would I add this to my life if it wasn't already there?*

If the answer is no, remove it.

Stop filling your calendar with tasks that feel productive but do not actually move your life forward. Stop saying yes to things out of obligation. Stop committing to things that do not align with what actually matters to you.

Your time should reflect your values, not just your responsibilities. Your calendar should be a reflection of what you want to build, not just a record of what you agreed to out of habit.

Every unnecessary commitment you eliminate gives you back energy, focus, and clarity. Every pointless obligation you cut makes space for what actually matters.

If your time is not intentionally designed, it will be consumed by everything except what is important to you. Take control of it now.

The End of the Detox—What Happens Next

At the end of this process, you will not just feel lighter. You will understand, maybe for the first time, how much unnecessary weight you were carrying.

The goal is not to eliminate everything and live in a state of perfect balance. The goal is to create space for what actually matters—without the distractions, obligations, and burdens that have been silently robbing you of your energy.

Tomorrow, you will wake up, and your life will look the same. But you? You will not feel the same.

Because you will know that this time, every thought, every commitment, every relationship, and every piece of your life is there because you chose it.

And that? That is the most manageable life you could ever ask for.

JOURNEY JOTS

Quick, thoughtful notes that document milestones, insights, and personal growth

JOURNEY JOTS

*Quick, thoughtful notes that document milestones,
insights, and personal growth*

_____

_____

_____

_____

_____

_____

_____

_____

_____

_____

_____

_____

_____

_____

_____

JOURNEY JOTS

Quick, thoughtful notes that document milestones,
insights, and personal growth

_____

_____

_____

_____

_____

_____

_____

_____

_____

_____

_____

_____

_____

_____

_____

_____

Postlude

Life is a breath—taken in gasps, in sighs, in quiet inhales of wonder. It is the weight of love pressed into our palms, the sharp sting of loss slipping through our fingers.

We are here for only a moment, luminous and fleeting, burning with the echoes of those before us. The world does not pause when we go, but the footprints we leave may linger—soft, fading, but never forgotten.

And when the last light dims, let it not be with regret, but with the quiet knowing: I was here. I mattered. I was enough.

Mantra:

"I was here. I mattered. I was enough."

www.ingramcontent.com/pod-product-compliance
Lightning Source LLC
Chambersburg PA
CBHW071731120626
46550CB00002B/484